Darkside Zodiac

at Work

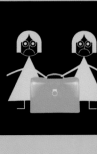

Darkside Zodiac
at Work

Stella Hyde

Illustrated by
Tonwen Jones

Ⓠ WEISER BOOKS
San Francisco, CA / Newburyport, MA

First published in 2007 by
Red Wheel/Weiser, LLC
500 Third Street, Suite 230
San Francisco, CA 94107
www.redwheelweiser.com

ISBN-10: 1-57863-402-4
ISBN-13: 978-1-57863-402-6

The dates for the zodiac signs in this book follow accepted standards, but people born at the beginning
or end of a sign should always check their birthchart; for technical, star-based reasons, the start and end
dates occasionally shift one day either way (and sometimes more), depending on the year.

This book was conceived, designed, and produced by iBall, an imprint of
IVY PRESS
The Old Candlemakers,
West Street, Lewes,
East Sussex, BN7 2NZ

Creative Director *Peter Bridgewater*
Publisher *Jason Hook*
Editorial Director *Caroline Earle*
Senior Project Editor *Dominique Page*
Art Director *Sarah Howerd*
Designer *Jane Lanaway*
Concept Design and Illustrator *Tonwen Jones*
Project Designer *Joanna Clinch*

Printed in Thailand

contents

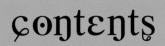

Introduction	6	
Caution: Planets at Work	8	
Working Through The Signs	**16**	
Aries	18	
Taurus	30	
Gemini	42	
Natural Born Bosses	54	
Cancer	60	
Leo	72	
Virgo	84	
Natural Born Middle Management	96	
Libra	102	
Scorpio	114	
Sagittarius	126	
Natural Born Slackers	138	
Capricorn	144	
Aquarius	156	
Pisces	168	
Instant Career Selector	182	
Further Reading	188	
Index	190	
Acknowledgments	192	

introduction

gray-sky thinking

Most of us spend most of our lives at work, and what help do we get to survive? Just a lot of mumbo about lactic product location, and how tidying your desk will lead to a seat on the board. It's not like that in the real world of work: accurate information is the key to success, so here is the skinny on what your work colleagues are really like, according to their Sun sign, so that you can defend yourself, attack their weak points, and predict their strategies. All you need to know is their birthday, and you can find that out by raiding the company database. I am contractually obliged to tell you that, as a Darkside product, this book contains harsh statements and strong language with which you may not be comfortable.

Qualities, elements, and opposites

Key astrological factors in the workplace are qualities and elements (bet you didn't think the zodiac had its own management-speak). There are three qualities that the zodiac will accept: cardinal (boss), fixed (middle management), and mutable (slacker), and these are partnered with four elements (Fire, Air, Earth, and Water); the shift patterns have been timetabled so that each quality gets to work with each element only once, and this combination is assigned to one particular Sun sign. This manual takes three comfort breaks, in which the quality/ element partnering dynamic is rigorously workshopped. To find out more, go to Natural Born Bosses (*page 54*), Natural Born Middle Management (*page 96*), and Natural Born Slackers (*page 138*).

There is also a briefing on your opposite sign, the celestial equivalent of your opposite number in Anchorage when you are in Key West. Just as in real life, you suspect they are after your job; find out how on pages 14–15.

Checklist

- Required personality profile, skill levels, and essential qualifications (opening job description)
- Work–life balance status (Workaholics)
- Remuneration deliverables (Show me the money)
- Unauthorized downtime variables (Excuses, excuses)
- Overall approach and attitude to work (The daily grind)
- Ergonomic environment ([insert sign here] workstation)
- Employability quotient (How employable are you?)
- Punctuality skills (Bad timing)
- Self-referred sick leave (Mental health day count)
- Suitable posts (Dream jobs)
- Aspirational avatars (Role model)
- Intrapersonal synergy (Office politics)
- Conflict resolution solutions (Backstabbing)

- Advancement strategies (You and the greasy pole)
- Informal information harvesting techniques (Watercooler moment)
- Sycophantic status (Brown-nose index)
- Positive proactive cooperation (Office fun)
- Nonessential colleague relationships (Office romance)
- Sanctioned variations in the sartorial paradigm (Dress-down disaster)
- Compulsory workplace socializing (Office party)
- Inappropriate interaction (Your cheapest trick)
- Positive collaborative action (Teamwork)
- Ranking status options (Leader, follow, passenger, grunt)
- Communication skills (Are you talking to me?)
- Co-sign interface dynamic (Worst-case scenario)
- Intersign interface dynamic (Know your enemies)

How to use this book

For each sign there is a rigorous assessment check, covering all significant aspects of work and workplace interaction. In accordance with Best Practice Guidelines for Transparency in the Work Environment, a checklist is provided above indicating each sign's performance levels.

Caution: Planets at Work

It's not all about the signs. The workplace has its own planetary board: Saturn, the boss; Mars, the CEO; and Mercury, the communications strategist. Regardless of your Sun sign, these three make a deep impact on life in the workplace. Find out what it is they actually do on the following pages. (To comply with health and safety regulations, a guide to Opposite Signs and how they can make a dull day worse is included in this section.)

Saturn

planet work

The Sun is, of course, the president of the zodiac, but Saturn is the boss, the grown-up planet that keeps the rest of the zodiac's nose to the grindstone and calls time on excess fun. I am not making this up; even Brightsiders call Saturn the Celestial Taskmaster.

Before there were telescopes, Saturn was the furthest planet that anyone could see with the naked eye—there was not a lot of ambient light around then, and there was no so much to do in the evening. It was considered to be the Great Limiter, the guardian of the solar system's perimeter. Down here, it's all about discipline, structure, focus, deadlines, more discipline, goal-oriented self-programming, the bottom line, maintaining budgetary parameters, and plenty of hard graft.

Officially Saturn is Capricorn's line manager, but in practice it bosses all of us about. Saturn spends around two and a half years on secondment in each sign, imposing new rules, downsizing, repurposing, reprioritizing, and generally making things leaner and meaner for the permanent staff. At the time of writing it is in Leo, forcing Lions to stop playing make-believe, and after September 2007 it will be in Virgo, forcing the lint-pickers to focus on the bigger picture. If you want to get ahead of the curve and be just a little bit of a smug teacher's pet, then check up how Saturn will affect you on any of the websites provided (*see page 189*).

The real Saturn

Actual planet Saturn is the sixth rock from the Sun, the large (but not as large as Jupiter) dignified one, banded with the rings of office that show just who is in executive command around here. It is accompanied by a Grade 1 personal secretary (the moon Titan) and by 22 administrative assistants (a bunch of smaller moons), so it is not so much a planet as a corporation. Saturn is named for a pre-Roman god who taught humanity how to plow and was actually quite fun, with his own week-long and extremely raunchy midwinter festival (Saturnalia), so obviously he had the whole work–life balance thing nailed; but Saturn later became associated with Cronos (due to an administrative snafu confusing it with *chronos*, meaning time). Cronos was the scary son of Oeranus, whom he castrated in order to get his hands on power. He also ate his own children (the Olympic gods) to prevent them taking power. Saturn means business.

Saturn returns

The Saturn trading year is 29½ Earth years—the time it takes to go around the Sun and return to its original position in our birth chart. It comes back into our lives when we are around 30 and 60, just as we think we might bust out in a different direction, to point out the restrictive clauses in our contracts.

This also means that when we are around 15, 45, and 75, Saturn is as far away from us as it can get, which explains adolescent slacking, the midlife crisis, and third-agers who get up one day and take the RV on the road to spend the kids' inheritance.

Mars

competitive edgy

On the positive side, Mars is all about your can-do approach to work, the energy levels you can be bothered to summon up to attack the daily piles of paperwork, and how loud you sing in the shower through sheer joy at the prospect of another eight hours at the coalface. On the Darkside, it's all about how psychotically competitive you are, what kind of bullying tactics you use, and whether you are actually, literally going to kill for that new contract.

Mars is like the hatchet wielder brought in by the organization to ginger up slack and complacent workforces. It takes about 2½ years to cover all of Zodiac, Inc., spending about two months piling on the pressure and clipping on the electrodes on each department in turn, which is just about as much as anyone can take, and far too long when it is in Aries or Scorpio.

Mars and you

Officially, Mars is the line manager for Aries, its special protégé who can never escape; and it trained Scorpios so well it is now afraid of them, especially as they have an even more psycho master in Pluto. However, we all have Mars somewhere in our birthchart, itching for a fight and ready to kick coworkers off the ladder. Go to www.alabe.com to find out where yours is, then read the relevant sign to see how it might compromise your career.

The real Mars

Mars is the small, red, glowering planet that orbits just next door to us. It's named for the Roman god of war, a remix of an ancient agricultural god and the Greek god of war, Ares—recognized even on Olympus as a violent braggart with too many extra X chromosomes.

Mercury

communication breakdown

Mercury is essential to the workplace because it is the hyperactive CEO of communications, with a wide brief covering databases, travel, cellphones, contracts, and the IT department. Somehow it also manages to fit in its responsibilities as line manager for Gemini and Virgo, both obsessed with information gathering and dispersal. Small and fast, Mercury is the first rock from the Sun, which it whirls around in 88 days, but at a variable rate, popping in and out of signs every few days— sometimes just in one day—because it hates being pinned down. This explains the ebb and flow of information, misinformation, and disinformation experienced in any office.

And to make things worse, every four months or so Mercury throws a hissy fit, closes down all systems, and goes retrograde (backward to you).

Mercury retrograde

Three times a year Mercury goes retrograde. This means that for astronomical mathematical geeky reasons, it appears to go backward. It does this for three weeks, appears to stop, then takes another three weeks to bowl back to the place it started.

What happens down here is communication meltdown: nothing gets signed, payments go astray, servers crash, e-mails evaporate, text messages go to the wrong person, the Intranet hosts a glitch-fest, the keys to the executive washroom fall down the back of the filing cabinet. Any important decision will be rubbish because it will have been based on rubbish data, since a very tiny but immensely significant word (such as "not") got left out at the drafting stage and no one picked it up; and small print becomes illegible.

opposite numbers

the other side of darkness

Your opposite sign sits on the opposite side of the zodiac wheel, six signs away, giving you knowing looks. It's got your number, but you've got its—so there's no political toehold there. Brightsiders claim there is a strong complementary relationship between you and your opposite sign, especially at work, because you share the same type of energy quality (cardinal, fixed, or mutable). And it's true, you do.

Darksiders, however, maintain right back that this shared energy can only lead to friction, tension, unpleasantness, stalemates, and Mexican standoffs in the workplace, because you both understand each other too well and fix your sights on the same goal.

Checkmates

In case you don't know, these are how the signs link up in a spooky umbilical way:

Aries and Libra
Shared energy: cardinal

Taurus and Scorpio
Shared energy: fixed

Gemini and Sagittarius
Shared energy: mutable

Cancer and Capricorn
Shared energy: cardinal

Leo and Aquarius
Shared energy: fixed

Virgo and Pisces
Shared energy: mutable

Fatal attraction

Standoff on main street
Aries — Libra

The moment of truth
Scorpio
Taurus

Mr. Green and Mr. Purple
Sagittarius
Gemini

The root of all evil
Capricorn
Cancer

Feel the force
Aquarius
Leo

Getting hooked
Pisces
Virgo

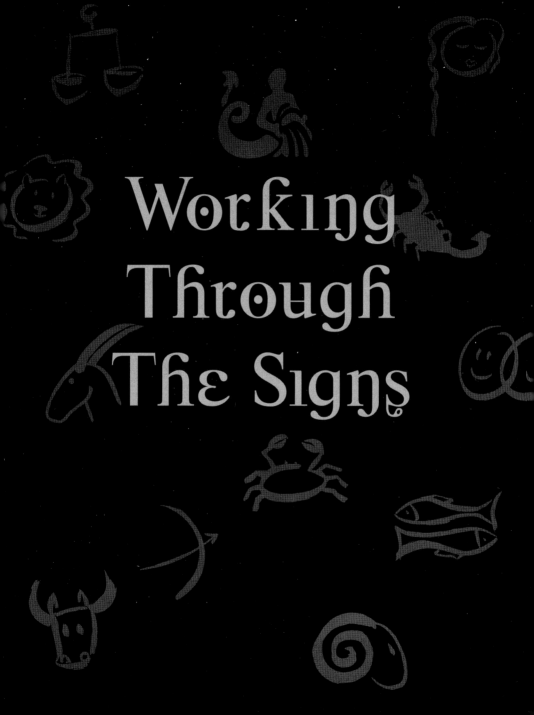

Working Through The Signs

Aries

March 21–April 20
Line Manager: Mars

Must be brash, crass and insensitive, confrontational, morbidly competitive, and pathologically incapable of being told what to do. Candidates should demonstrate robust bullying skills without discriminating in any way (the zodiac is an equal-opportunities employer). A juvenile criminal record (preferably arson and Grand Theft Auto) is desirable. Applicants are advised that a pushy, extrovert demeanor and a strong grip on the inner psychopath are core strengths, and special consideration will be given to candidates with short fuses and above-average levels of recklessness and irritability. Those who have been fired from several jobs consecutively will have an advantage, as will those who have failed at least two anger-management courses.

Workaholics

Certainly not. You don't have the necessary attention span to take the office home with you. You'd rather spend more time with your Porsche Spyder, PlayStation®, or someone else's partner.

Show me the money

You have drawn so many salary advances you now owe the company 10 years of your life. You wish they would pay you in cash, then at least you could get to see what you were burning.

Excuses, excuses

You'd rather infect the whole multicorp than call in sick and miss a day's in-fighting. You pack industrial-strength Advil® to combat the raging headaches usually brought on by—er, rage.

the daily grind

my way or nothing

Some of the workforce simply will not follow your orders without question. All right, you are "only" the janitor, but is that the point? Obviously you know better than anyone else how to do the job—any job—even though you have no experience and have never even seen the flight controls of a stealth bomber before. You work on the principle that shouting with confidence and acting aggressive are the answer to everything, and the sad thing is you are mostly always right. Myopic employers hire you for your energy, direction, and drive. They never ask themselves why, if you're as hot as you think you are, you're so available? Once in charge, you crash around, alienating the workforce and gleefully tearing down all of the old systems, but not putting anything in their place, because that would be boring and you don't do detail. You usually get paid off handsomely before writs are served. Astute employers hire you to run down perfectly viable companies for barely legal tax reasons. When you are fired, you don't bother with lawsuits and conciliation services—you just sneak around on a dark night with a Molotov cocktail and torch the place.

Aries workstation

Hot-desking was your invention because you could never find your workstation under the clutter. The office feng shui sensei had to be rushed to Emergency Reflexology when she saw it. You claim it is to combat industrial espionage by installing controlled chaos.

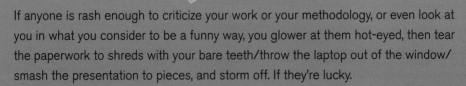

If anyone is rash enough to criticize your work or your methodology, or even look at you in what you consider to be a funny way, you glower at them hot-eyed, then tear the paperwork to shreds with your bare teeth/throw the laptop out of the window/ smash the presentation to pieces, and storm off. If they're lucky.

Bad timing

You put in the hours (if there's one thing you're not, it's lazy) —they're just not the same as everyone else's. You are either fighting past night security at four in the morning with a hot new scheme or untraceable. You don't do presenteeism.

How employable are you?

Office life isn't really you, is it? Routine? I don't think so. Paperwork? You know what happens when fire meets paper—and it's no better electronically: you crash the system, head-butt the monitor, and use the mouse as a bolas to bring down enemies. Don't even think of the caring professions—you won't afford the negligence lawsuits; anything involving empathy, a steady hand, or a cool aim is also out. Best work outdoors, on your own with big, strong tools that don't break down easily.

Mental health day count

Low. You despise weakness and would rather come in and make everyone else suffer.

Dream jobs for Aries

So what should you do in the ideal Arien world of work? What would suit you best and inflict the least harm on everyone else?

Lone explorer

Fantastic! Be the first to hack your way through virgin rainforest, scale an unclimbed alp, or cross an uncharted desert. Spit in the face of caution and local advice. Get sent home in a bodybag.

Firefighter

Fire, danger, big sharp axes, shiny red appliances to ride on—and the chance to be everybody's hero. Resist the temptation to start the odd conflagration just because the day's a bit slow.

Role model

Leonardo da Vinci (April 15, 1452). The original Renaissance man, bursting with new ideas, but not a slave to detail (or finishing anything), and just a speck in the distance when anybody asked questions like, "How exactly does this flying machine work, then, Leo?" Your kind of guy.

Leonardo da Vinci

office politics

who's hidden the agenda?

You have a refreshingly simple view of life (you are the leader, everybody does what you say) and can do very well in macho environments (the Killing Floor, NYSE trading pits, the White House press corps) where brute force, raw energy, unassailable self-belief, and very sharp elbows are all assets. Subtleties fly right over your horns. If someone's hidden the agenda, surely we can just print up a copy, you fume. You don't understand all the fuss about the executive washroom (you'll go anywhere), and always storm impatiently out of board meetings before it gets to the interesting who-will-shaft-who part. You think, smugly, that you are a good judge of ally; you don't realize that your allies choose you, mainly for your brute force, energy, elbows, etc.

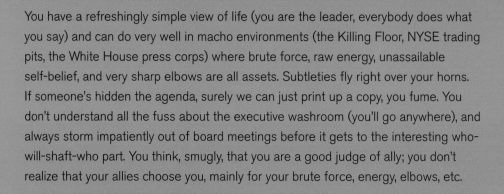

Backstabbing

Not your forte; think about it—you would have to let someone else get in front of you in order to stab them in the back, and that's a strategy too far for your simple Arien brain. Head-to-head confrontation is more your style; you like your fighting out in the open.

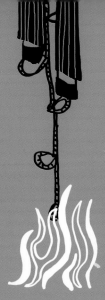

You and the greasy pole

You adore a challenge and thrive in high places, so are rather good at clattering your way up the career ladder. You don't waste time worrying about what you don't understand, obsessing about detail, or finessing a complicated self-advancement scheme for so long that it becomes obsolete. Sometimes the simplest ways are the best. You make so much impatient noise that people quietly enjoying the view on higher rungs simply move over to let you through so they can get some peace. There's only room on your ladder for you, and you burn it as you go, so that no one can follow you up.

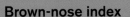

Brown-nose index

Around zero. Not only do you not put in any boss-oiling hours, you never hesitate to point out where he or she is wrong and you are right. You can't even spot the strategic players in Office Games, let alone buy them candy or cigars.

Watercooler moment

You love it at the watercooler: it's where the flock gathers, so you can show them who's leader of the pack—and you do like to make waves.

offiçε fun

all play and no work …

Because you suffer from chronic LBT (Low Boredom Threshold), you are constantly looking for more interesting ways to pass the time while you are imprisoned in your work pod. Naive managements think you are a morale-raising godsend, until they get the month's productivity figures in. You are no slacker, and you bring to office fun and games all the unstoppable ambition and competitive edge that you apply (in very short bursts) to actual work; Sagittarians may start up Extreme Office Sports, but you are the one who takes it global and organizes the Office Olympics. And practical jokes are always good for relieving tension, aren't they? You are especially proud of the whoopee cushions you smuggled into that high-level deal-breaking meeting.

Office romance

You are the office Casanova (one of your sign mates, after all); the challenge is irresistible, the risk factor thrillingly high. You're not after power and you don't work on the casting-couch principle, you just love the buzz of getting it on in edgy venues (the CEO's Lexus, the glass elevator in the atrium, under the boardroom table at the AGM) with someone new. You try to stay friends afterward, because it was nothing personal, but you get bored if asked for repeat performances.

Dress-down disasters

Deprived of the office uniform, which you secretly love, you dress in whatever comes to hand, which could mean golf pants, cowboy boots, and the Ramones T-shirt you found in the back of the closet. This only works if you're a babe or the cute new mailboy, but you don't care.

Office party

Formal office parties bore you rigid, and you don't hesitate to say so—loudly—offering to organize a much more fun event, viz. a paintballing weekend. Your team (you and a couple of Sagittarians) is always the last one left unbeaten in the woods when everyone else has gone home to bathe in a large Martini. You'll never understand why no one else but you paintballed the boss.

Your cheapest trick

You are not one for complicated, cerebral, bitchy scams involving e-mails or IT; slapstick and old-school practical jokes are what you do best, and no one can stop you. Covering a grouchy colleague's cubicle with sticky notes, gluing all the mice to their mousemats, filling the watercooler with fake blood …

teamwork

red leader one

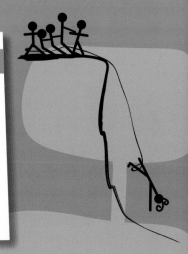

"There's no 'I' in teamwork"—what does that mean exactly? There's no "R" either—duh. You are mystified (but if you are a smart Ram, you could point out that there is one in "cooperation"). Actually you quite like to work with a team (or "platoon"), as long as you can be team leader. Other signs find it quite restful, because you put in all the energy; besides, if you are not team leader, you sulk like Achilles in his tent, and nobody can bear the tension. Anyone who challenges your leadership is welcome to step outside. You never drop any team member in it—at least not on purpose (although any halfway smart boss can guess who the deadweight is by your tactless chatter)—but they will suffer later from a series of bizarre stapler-related accidents.

Leader, follower, passenger, grunt

Leader, natch—even if it does mean dragging the company with you over the cliff. Forced into a follower niche, you argue furiously with the poor sap who is the leader, disrespect their authority, and shunt the entire project off-script. If the leader is another Arien, the entire department is doomed. You can't sit still long enough to be a passenger and totally fail to see its advantages (reward without responsibility). However, you make quite a good grunt, at least for a few weeks, until you form a guerrilla team of other disaffected grunts and annex the executive dining room in a textbook *coup de bureau*.

Know your enemies

Aries—a cardinal Fire sign, just like you; that's not going to work, is it?

Taurus—will bring you down with the twin weapons of routine and more routine.

Gemini—hacks into your computer and sends rude e-mails from your account.

Cancer—a cardinal Water sign; and what does water do to fire?

Leo—the fixed Fire sign, will put out your fire by roaring even louder.

Virgo—buries your every executive action in triplicate paperwork.

Libra—your opposite sign, so everything that you're not; will beat you with guile.

Scorpio—your best friend when needing muscle to back up their mind games.

Sagittarius—the mutable Fire sign, will kick up a dust to extinguish your flame.

Capricorn—stops you in your tracks just by refusing to sanction your expenses.

Aquarius—speaks in jargon, knowing you don't have the patience to decode it.

Pisces—you're always the bigger boy that Pisces says made them do it.

Are you talking to me?

Communication is a one-way street for Ariens. You shout, you assume they listen, and you always work on a need-to-know basis. As far as you're concerned, no one needs to know anything except you. It's megaphone diplomacy, without the diplomacy bit.

Worst-case scenario

From the company's POV, a team full of Ariens automatically means higher insurance premiums (especially for fire), some serious hedge funding, and a red-hot libel lawyer on retainer. A couple of strategically placed Virgos should curb excess Ram enthusiasm.

Taurus

ℹ️ April 2–May 20
Line Manager: Venus

Exceptionally pig-headed levels of obstinacy and complete lack of spontaneity are essential for this position, and an inability to adapt to circumstances is a positive advantage. Applicants are advised that intractable recalcitrance and jealous resentment will be perceived as core strengths, with special consideration shown to those possessing unshakeable self-belief in the face of overwhelming contrary evidence. Fear of compromise and periodic bouts of murderous rage are no barrier to advancement, as the zodiac operates a Positive Discrimination Policy. Candidates should have majored in Stubborn Studies and demonstrate a near-paranoid obsession with money and possessions. Stupefying dullness is encouraged. Multitaskers need not apply.

Workaholics

Just because you show up every day doesn't mean you have to take an interest. You would never dream of taking the office home with you, as that would upset the routine you have at home.

Show me the money

Oh yes; never mind any of the objectives, prioritize the paycheck. It's the first thing you negotiate, and the only reason you do any work; if you could get it upfront in solid gold coins, you would.

Excuses, excuses

You lack the imagination to call in "sick," but may have to stay in the paddock sometimes, with a sore throat from too much bellowing, or unspecified bilious attacks.

comatose   laid-back   hands off   hands on   hands round   control   out-of-control

tɦe ɗaɪʟy gɾɪŋɗ

meal ticket

You would not miss the nobility of work if the Bad Fairy swung it so that you could have all the money for none of the effort. Standing around in fields chewing is, after all, what you do best. However, unless born rich (and you make a great famous-for-being-famous celebrity shopaholic), you are also boringly realistic. This means you will do more or less anything as long as it does not involve rapid response, getting grimy, or having to adjust on the hoof to moving goal posts, and there is a good company cafeteria. People soon stop asking for a decision—unless they have a month hidden in the schedule—or suggesting that you do anything not specified in your job description. Of course you join your trade union; restrictive practices are so you. Employers are impressed at first because you positively embrace mind-numbing routine. They promote you; you demand a salary hike. They laugh; you point out clause 287b (ii) in your contract. They prevaricate; you take them to cumulative industrial tribunals and eventually the Supreme Court, wiping out company profits at a stroke. Result! You are fireproof.

Taurus workstation

A Taurean's territory is sacred. Colleagues soon learn not to step over the invisible border between their workstation and yours; never to rearrange the icons on your desktop; and never to use your Special Mug. You think no one knows about your other secret chocolate drawer.

If anyone criticizes your work or your work rate you point out calmly that you were only following orders; if they no longer want what they once wanted, that is not your problem. And no force in the zodiac is going to up your plod rate, unless a particularly delicious toreador passes with a sackload of cowcake. Then you are unstoppable.

Bad timing

You always arrive precisely on time, effortlessly ruining everyone else's day, but you will also stop working precisely on time, even if the brain surgery has reached that delicate stage where the eyeballs have to be put back in.

How employable are you?

Very; you appear neat, tidy, punctual, and reliable—and worryingly unsackable. You are always ready to follow orders (however dumb) and, even better, to bellow them on to subordinates. That's a set of transferable skills you don't often meet in the zodiac, and the joy is they can be applied to almost all jobs (clerk, insurance agent, realtor, torturer)—as long as you steer clear of anything vocational or demanding a social conscience. Best work indoors, with a herd, doing something unexciting.

Mental health day count

Low. Your routine would go to pot, and you only suffer that murderous psychotic rage-thing twice a year anyway.

Dream jobs for Taurus

So what should you do in the ideal Taurean world of work? What would suit you best and inflict the least harm on everyone else?

Asset stripper

Your ability to spot a wounded beast, bargain, and a money-making opportunity—coupled with your genuine insensitivity to job losses, starving families, and senior-citizen suicides—makes this a bull's eye.

Genghis Khan

Real estate tycoon

We see industrial wasteland; you see shopping malls and executive apartments. We see undeveloped fishing villages; you see high-return executive summer rentals. We see unspoiled wilderness; you see a prairie full of cash cows.

Role model

Genghis Khan (May 5 c. 1152). The world dictator's world dictator; Khan means universal ruler. Took over the Mongol Horde when he was only 13 and slowly but surely built up a huge piece of imperial real-estate that stretched from the Black Sea to the Pacific. Serious bulling.

office politics

who moved my cake?

You are easily bedazzled by the web of plots and counterplots hurled around you by the zodiac's spinmeisters, but you put your head down and hold on to what really matters to you—like who's got the biggest desk and the fattest expense account, and how you can get them. You can't begin to second-guess your enemies because you simply do not have the imagination to think out their next move. However, you are really good at standing still for long periods, saying nothing, and pawing the ground a bit (metaphorically speaking). This makes you appear powerful and dangerous, and, as long as you don't actually take any action, you often find yourself the winner in departmental shootouts without knowing how.

Backstabbing

This is a bit subtle for you, plus it's hard to hold a stiletto in a cloven hoof. You prefer the full-frontal attack: trampling underfoot (preferably while wearing your Manolo alligator boots), or a public goring in the arena of your choice (although you don't always win this one).

You and the greasy pole

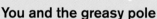

Bulls are not really built to go up stairs, and you would prefer to cover the miles on the flat than get vertigo trying to climb—but hey, if Swiss cows can scale mountains, you'll give it a try. (Swiss cows must have an edge: they know about money and chocolate.) However, you move really slowly, testing the rungs at each stage, and tend to reach the top just as the founder's granddaughter takes over the company and sells it. People behind you can't push past or go around, so usually leave and start a whole new empire.

Brown-nose index

You plod in at about three on the scale. You can never think of anything smarmy to say to the boss, so don't say anything. Luckily for you, bosses often mistake bovine silence for dumb loyalty, so you end up with a company car or a pay rise anyway.

Watercooler moment

You think the watercooler is where you go to get drinks of water. You have a regular watercooler slot, and you always go at that time, regardless of whether there is anyone there to talk to or not.

offiçe fun

comic routine

It's a bit difficult for you to have fun during working hours—not because you don't want to, but because that would mean having to think about more than one thing at a time. The rest of the sales team may have to wait a few hours for you to get up to frolic speed, but after that there's no stopping you. You've got your three jokes (the ones you always tell because you've always told them) and turn up at the usual office watering hole every Friday, ready for Designated Fun Hour, even when everyone else has moved on to the hot new Latino bar three blocks away. There is a card saying "You don't have to be mad to work here, but it helps" stuck neatly on the wall of your cubicle. It never fails to make you smile.

Office romance

You may be the Duke or Duchess of Dull, but you report upline to Venus, CEO of the Lust and Having It Department, so are likely to be the Office Lech. It often ends in injunctions, because you won't take no for an answer, but, as you're quite cute, you succeed just by standing there. Your affairs are never secret, as you insist on meeting at the same time every week, and think that getting jiggy with it on the photocopier is a novel notion.

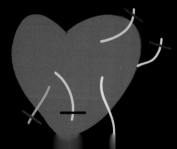

Dress-down disasters

Dress down means dress up for you—a chance to show off your second-best bling, your new Choos, and the tight leather skirt/pants. This is not the best look if you're a firefighter or lifeguard, but them's the rules, and you love rules.

Office party

You come into your own at the office party. Who would have thought you could put away so many canapés and down quite so many mojitos. It's like watching mild-mannered Clark Kent turn into Extreme Eating Man. You always stay right to the end, and help the caterers by taking home the leftover cases of Shiraz. You loathe bonding weekends: there may not be enough food.

Your cheapest trick

You don't think quickly enough to fool cube-mates with witty wind-ups. Your idea of fun is to swipe all the donuts, eat them, then pretend you haven't, despite the sugar around your mouth. It's as if Steve Martin's actually in the room! Of course, if someone steals your donuts, you gore them with your Mont Blanc.

teamwork

plowing on

In the beginning, everyone thinks of you as a great team player: the solid reliable fullback, who will carry the dull load, too unimaginative to complain or think of a get-out clause. Then they find out you play the same game plan you always play, regardless of the game; are incapable of on-the-hoof improvisation when thrown a curveball; and will stop the operation in its tracks by refusing to change direction. You have no interest in other team members' plans to improve performance unless they are exactly the same as yours; the "vision thing" is not really you—you can only see as far as the end of your own field. While you're not the company snitch, you don't see why you shouldn't tell it like it is, especially if there's a reward.

Leader, follower, passenger, grunt

Moving slowly along with a crowd of followers is your default mode, but the rest of the zodiac should remember that bulls are put in fields on their own for a good reason. Some of you have long, slow bully dreams about the day you will be team leader—then they will have to do it your way. Fortunately your plan usually involves nothing more than waiting for the bull in front to drop dead. You put in too many hours to be a passenger, but can be the perfect grunt if the money's good enough.

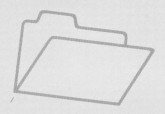

Know your enemies

Aries—stand still and chew, with your iPod on max; they'll soon give up shouting at you.

Taurus—a fixed Earth sign, just like you; who's going to give the required inch?

Gemini—teases you in meetings by changing the agenda at the last minute.

Cancer—the constant mood swinging gives you a migraine, so you concede the game.

Leo—the fixed Fire sign; they can barbecue you in an instant, so you do what they say.

Virgo—mutable Earth sign, so has more impressive routines than you do.

Libra—shares your line manager (Venus) and is so much smarter at manipulating her.

Scorpio—your opposite sign, everything you're not—the matador to your bull.

Sagittarius—wastes energy running around you in circles, so you win in the end.

Capricorn—the cardinal Earth sign, so has a higher Inflexibility Quotient than you.

Aquarius—loads you up with carbs before that crucial presentation; you can't resist.

Pisces—messes up the mission, but blames you; you are too slow to get out of the way.

Are you talking to me?

When you have something to say, you say it. If someone asks you to explain what you mean, you simply say it again, bellowing. Feedback confuses you; you don't really understand what it's for, because there's no way you're going to adapt the plan.

Worst-case scenario

From the company's POV, a team of Taureans will only work if yoked together in line; otherwise your separate Obstinacy Drives will plow the whole business into the ground. A Gemini overseer will annoy the team into moving faster.

Gemini

♊

May 21–June 20
Line Manager: Mercury

Candidates should demonstrate a consistently high pitch of inconsistency, dissatisfaction, and restlessness, and produce references (showing professional levels of signature forgery) to back up any self-certified claims to unreliability. There will be an oral assessment in which applicants are expected to prove that white is black and to impersonate three of the interviewing panel well enough to fool the head of security. By the end of the session the applicant should have lifted six major credit cards, two BlackBerries, and a Rolex. Superficiality is regarded as a core strength. Nimble fingers will be an advantage, and people with a fully functioning conscience need not apply. Applicants who can certify broad spectrum **ADHD** will be given preference.

Workaholics

Oh, please. As if you'd let work interfere with your constant Rolling Vacation Program. But, of course, you look the part, always on your cellphone or flipping through your Rolodex.

Show me the money

It's a challenge for you if the paycheck isn't worth getting out of bed for: you can spend your working hours inventing fake expenses and flogging the newer office hardware on eBay.

Excuses, excuses

You're not sick, you're just attending the funeral of your deceased grandmother, yet again. You sometimes call in with a hand injury, sustained when snatching it out of the cash register too quickly.

comatose   laid-back   hands off   hands on   hands around   control   out of control

the daily grind

would I lie to you?

Your native instinct to deceive means that you thrive in any workplace—it doesn't matter what kind, although your quick, shiny little mind means you are a natural for all those jobs requiring a sociopathic ability to lie without contradiction or feeling ashamed of yourself: lawyering, advertising, PR, customer relations. You can con your way into almost any position—what do a few boring qualifications that no one is going to check matter? It's only brain surgery. Once hired, you gravitate effortlessly toward the influential people, where you ingratiate yourself with shameless fawning and flattery. You're also cunning enough to pinpoint key personnel lower down the food chain (doorman, receptionist, accounts clerk, janitor), whom you can bedazzle into submission without even breaking sweat, and who will eagerly hand over all the information you need to apply a little extra leverage in just the right place when your six-monthly review comes around. You burn a lot of energy arranging things so that you get maximum reward for minimum effort. You'd never just do the work instead—where's the fun in that?

Gemini workstation

Smooth talking to the feng shui consultant means your basecamp is the one nearest the only natural light source, and protected from the Poisoned Arrows coming from other stations by a higher-than-usual screen. Your desk is littered with gadgets, very few of which are yours.

If anyone calls your bluff (it was careless of you to lift that presentation from the sap you are romancing at a rival agency), you lawyer up (preferably another Gemini), sue for mental cruelty, and win compensation. If the boss threatens you with the chop, you smile and wonder dreamily (out loud) if they have looked on their hard drive lately.

Bad timing

You like to get in nice and early, so you can get at everyone else's e-mails. After that, Accounts think you are in Sales; Sales think you are in HR; HR think you are in Accounts. You invented the jacket-on-the-back-of-the-chair trick.

How employable are you?

Extremely so—in fact you usually have four or five jobs on the go at once. (Webmail is a godsend.) For a high return from zero effort, you slide into Sales, where you shift warehouseloads of ice-making machines to your rival's Alaskan subsidiary; it gets you a fat bonus, or into Public Relations, where you spin that disastrous oil spill into a charitable eco-scheme to waterproof the Venezuelan coastline. No sane CEO will let you near the company finances, but that doesn't mean you won't get there.

Mental health day count

Another one of your inventions, which, of course, you're smart enough not to overuse.

Dream jobs for Gemini

So what should you do in the ideal Geminian world of work? What would suit you best and inflict the least harm on everyone else?

Gawker content manager

Digging dirt, spreading ugly rumors, reading other people's mail, inventing bitchy names, scouring the Web for gossip, and getting paid to do what you do for free anyway.

Che Guevara

Spy

As you have no moral perceptions, it really doesn't matter whose side you're on—it's the game you love: inventing bogus info and outwitting the slow. You might get shot, but that just makes it a bit more sexy.

Role model

Of course, you can have two, one for each twin: Che Guevara (June 14, 1928), restless, romantic multitasker (doctor, revolutionary, soldier); and DC Comics' Superman (early June 1938), restless, fictional mega-multitasker (Clark Kent, journalist, and superhero).

offiçe polıtıçs

the West Wing called—they want you back

You patrol the choppy waters of office politics like a shark stalking surfers, and with the same wide toothy smile. Your weapon of choice is gossip, the easy option for an Olympic-class, two-faced dirt-disher like you. A nugget of disinformation here, an innuendo there, a bunch of accidentally forwarded e-mails, some misdirected txt msgs, careless whispers to taste, and pretty soon there's a fine little feud brewing. But everyone still loves you. It's uncanny how you can pick up on the buddy patterning in any group of people; you like to keep boredom at bay by getting A to do anything you want them to do by manipulating B, whom they loathe, into begging them not to do it. Sometimes it's just all too easy.

Backstabbing

You are so good at this that many of your victims don't even feel the pain, until Security are escorting them off the premises. Ruthless CEOs who hire you for this reason have only themselves to blame when you skewer them. Iago is one of your role models, after all.

You and the greasy pole

You shin up the work ladder like a monkey up a coconut palm, oiling the rungs with wit, charm, and blackmail as you go. You are devastated if anyone falls off as you pass. "How could that have happened?" you cry, sliding the tripwire back into your secret pocket. When you reach the top, the view is boring, so you grab the jungle vine you made earlier in Networking 101 and swing across to the slightly taller, but more stylish ladder of the hot new company that you've been moonlighting with for the past month.

Brown-nose index

Top of the scale at 11, as good as Libra, but extra stars for added subtlety. No loud, ingratiating laughter at the boss's jokes or turning up in the same-color shirt, but plenty of Body Language Mirroring to show that you are sympatico and have a totally coincidental addiction to Coldplay/ The Yankees/American Idol.

Watercooler moment

This is an ideal habitat for you, as magnetic as an antelope's watering hole is to a cheetah—with much the same result.

office fun

betcha by golly, wow

Life is one big game to you, and work is just part of the game, with slightly modified rules. Bedazzled by your patter and sincere smile (unless on the end of one of your outrageous scams), your colleagues are grateful to you for livening up the long and tedious day; you take the credit, but do it to entertain yourself, otherwise you might get bored. Fortunately e-fun (what is e-mail, if not a perfect opportunity to gossip in silence?) has made things even better. You have patented software that activates a convincing spreadsheet screensaver at the push of a spacebar (or via your cellphone when away from your desk flirting) to cover up your lucrative online poker habit. You should not be allowed to run the office sweepstake.

Office romance

As the zodiac's love rat and commitment-phobe, you welcome the office as another flirt arena. You can sweet-talk anybody into the utility cupboard with you; but a smooth operator like you needs a challenge, so it's a point of honor to blarney the mousy researcher out of his corner, or seduce the boss under the boardroom table. By the time you move on, you'll have had everyone who's not positively ugly, but because you're so cunning, none of them will know about the others.

Dress-down disasters

As it's Friday and you'll be weekending at the Hamptons, you come in looking like Ralph Lauren has sponsored your day. Next week it will be a tankini because you're flying to Acapulco, or a tight ski-bunny outfit because you're off to Aspen.

Office party

Oh yes, but you prefer a cocktail party to a sit-down dinner, because you can work the room and not get stuck next to the Office Bore. You always leave a few minutes after the important people, and snag a magnum or two to take with you to a more interesting party, with rock stars and a goat, at the other end of town. Bonding weekends let you show just how all-things-to-all-men a person can be.

Your cheapest trick

You are the zodiac's merry prankster. You specialize in stuff that has no comeback, because people feel so stupid falling for it that they won't challenge you—convincing a pushy overachiever that Bill Clinton's birthday is a national holiday, when you know it is the day of the big-deal meeting that will seal their fate ...

teamwork

two's company

"There's no we in team," you joke, although it usually falls flat. You mean it, though; you need the freedom to change horses in midstream, so you avoid all that bonding business. Your teammates love you because you tell such great jokes, but if you were bribed to throw the match, you wouldn't hesitate (unless it was to hustle for better terms). Ironically, you are worth your place in the squad, because you are fantastic at those Henry V-style, blood-stirring motivational speeches, delivered just before the boardroom battle, which you won't be able to fight as you have just remembered an emergency appointment with your parole officer. Of course you drop your best friend in the doo-doo; you can't help yourself.

Leader, follower, passenger, grunt

Your short attention span means you're not a natural leader. If in charge, you send everyone off in different directions at once. It is much more you to be a follower, especially with your sharply honed manipulating skills; it means that when it all goes wrong you don't have to carry the can. You are not indolent enough to be a full-time passenger, although you do like a regular catnap to recharge the fizzing batteries. If you are thrown in at the grunt end, it won't take you two seconds to raise consciousness and incite unrest. You'll have a revolution on your hands before you can say "Cuba Libre."

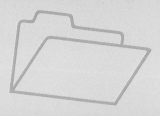

Know your enemies

Aries—they roar; you fan the flames with your witty sneers until they self-combust.

Taurus—no amount of barbed bitchery is going to make them pull in your direction.

Gemini—a mutable Air sign, just like you; two grifters, off to con the world.

Cancer—you know all moms forgive you anything, and Cancer is the zodiac's mom.

Leo—but the zodiac's dad is not about to increase your allowance or let you drive.

Virgo—shares your line manager, Mercury, so has been copied in to your agenda.

Libra—the cardinal Air sign, so you show a bit of respect and pick up some new tricks.

Scorpio—you move just too quickly for them to pin you down with their icy glare.

Sagittarius—your opposite sign, so everything you are, but without the finesse.

Capricorn—the only sign between you and the company filing for Chapter 11.

Aquarius—they know how to crash the system better than you do. Why don't they?

Pisces—you draw up a worthless contract, they sign under a false name. Stalemate.

Are you talking to me?

Communication is second nature to you, and you get bored waiting for dumbasses to get the message; that is why you invented Management Speak (you're very proud of Pushing the Envelope), and now wish you had taken out copyright on it.

Worst-case scenario

From the company's POV, a team of Geminis means an astronomical telecommunications budget and sackloads of pending writs and embezzlement raps. Together, a Taurus and a Capricorn may be able to flare off excess nervous excitement.

Aries

Cancer

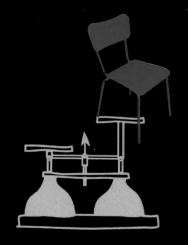

Libra

Capricorn

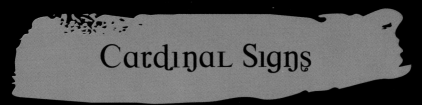

Cardinal Signs

Natural Born Bosses

If you have bothered to read the notes about qualities, elements, and opposites (*page 6*), you should be up to speed about the three qualities. In this little break from daily grind we are going to look at the cardinal quality—the one that, in theory, produces the Natural Born Boss.

Cardinal is from the Latin *cardo*, meaning hinge, and the cardinal signs are scheduled to come onstream at pivotal times in the year—the Spring and Fall equinoxes (Aries, Libra) and the Summer and Winter solstices (Cancer, Capricorn)—when the planets stand poised ready to plunge into some fresh hell. So cardinal signs are the initiators, the action-at-all-costs-and-I-don't-care-if-it-kills-me-and-any-number-of-innocent-bystanders kind. They set things in motion; it doesn't much matter what, because they won't be around to finish what they started; by the time the brown stuff hits the windmill, they are off being tiresomely entrepreneurial and fixing stuff that wasn't broke somewhere else.

This doesn't mean that everybody who is a boss is a cardinal sign, but every cardinal sign wants to be a boss, and behaves in a bossly way, even if they are only the doorman.

Aries cardinal fire

meet the new boss

Aries is the first cardinal sign, the initial sign on the zodiac wheel, and lines up with the Spring equinox. It's all about impatience, thrust, aggression, energy, and me-first. Don't you feel tired already?

The Aries boss surges into a new company after intimidating the board into employing them, sets about destroying all systems and infrastructure, fires the people who know what they're doing, and busts the budget headhunting a whole bunch of other people who will do what Aries wants. The company goes into meltdown, and Aries boss demands a golden handshake to go and energize someplace else.

Aries bosses

Russell Crowe
Diana Ross
Marlon Brando
Francis Ford Coppola

Fire

Aries is a Fire sign, Fire is the element of irreversible action (a.k.a. boat-burning), and cardinal Fire rages like an unpredictable active volcano. So the Aries boss is in a constant state of hot-tempered seethe, ready to blow at any moment, and demands action at all times, however pointless.

Mission statement

To boldly do it my way—and now.

Cancer cardinal water

mommy dearest

Cancer is the second cardinal sign, and lines up with the Summer solstice. Solstice means standing still, teetering on the point where going up meets coming down. It's all about passive-aggressive control.

The Cancer boss sidles into a company, usually by stealth or nepotism (how else did Dubya get to rule the world?), then spends serious desk time secretly panicking in case they: a) succeed or b) fail. The good-mom/bad-mom mood swings mean they constantly confuse the workforce by alternatively baking them cookies and then ordering them to clear their desks.

Water

Cancer is a Water sign, Water is the element of sentimental emotionalism, and cardinal Water is like an unstoppable geyser, turning the immediate area into an emotional bog. Anyone who comes near will get stuck and won't be able to leave until Cancer quits.

Mission statement

Committed to maintaining dependency across all sectors of industry.

Cancer bosses

George W. Bush
Donald Rumsfeld
Julius Caesar
Imelda Marcos

Libra cardinal air

velvet glove

Libra is the third cardinal sign, and lines up with the Fall equinox, the one that tips us into winter (at least in the northern hemisphere). It's the opposite sign to Aries, so is all about the creative power of doing as little as possible.

The Libran boss glides in on a cushion of charm, after oozing past the selection committee on a forged résumé and a smile, commissions a feasibility study on reform to assess the usefulness of nominating someone to set up a steering committee to elect an executive taskforce, then goes out to an upscale lunch with added retail therapy because they have worked so hard.

Libra bosses

Margaret Thatcher
Bruce Springsteen
Friedrich Nietzsche
Alfred Nobel

Air

Libra is an Air sign, Air is the element of intellect and communication (a.k.a. avoiding action by thinking about it instead), and cardinal Air is the source of the kind of high-powered hot air needed to do this. A Libran boss uses it to fuel their career balloon, which is why they feel constantly insecure.

Mission statement

Devolving power across the board, so can leave the office at 3:30.

Capricorn *cardinal earth*

keeping it real

Capricorn is the fourth cardinal sign, and lines up with the Winter solstice, at the bottom of the year when the only way is up. It's the opposite to Cancer, so is all about plain old aggressive control.

The Capricorn boss finally reaches the top of the corporate tree after years of graft, planning, butt-kissing, and treachery, and has brought their own safety harness in case of mutiny. Their first action is to audit the books to make sure their pension scheme is performing robustly, and their second action is to slash wages and budgets to make sure it continues to do so.

Earth

Capricorn is an Earth sign, Earth is the element of practical materialism, stuff you can get hold of, and cardinal Earth is primordial dirt—full of potential, but grubby-making. This means there is not much that the Capricorn boss won't do to stay on top.

Mission statement

To relentlessly chase the bottom line, no matter what the human cost.

Capricorn bosses

Elvis Presley

Hermann Göring

Al Capone

Josef Stalin

Cancer

⊙♋

June 21–July 22

Line Manager: Moon

An exceptional grasp of the futility of existence is essential in this post, as well as a Masters in Pointless Worrying. Negative levels of self-esteem are a basic requirement. Candidates should demonstrate advanced mood-changing skills, and show that they can infect a minimum of six surrounding workstations with paralyzing existential gloom. Applicants should supply their own exterior hard-drive for grudge storage. Although the zodiac endeavors to comply with international guidelines, this post is not currently available to persons with normal levels of serotonin, although Schadenfreude addicts with a history of failed rehabilitation are encouraged to apply. Candidates are reminded that they probably won't get the job anyway.

Workaholics

You may well take the office home with you, but you also bring home to the office: so you spend your days calling the cable guy or the car shop and your nights writing up monthly progress reports.

Show me the money

A fat paycheck may not be your only motivation, but since everyone is going to do you down, you check the small print closely with your beady little eyes and pull off surprisingly good deals.

Excuses, excuses

You rarely call in, because being slightly ill at work offers you some great martyring opportunities. If you are sick, it's usually a stress-related stomach-ache. Or hormones.

comatose   laid-back   *hands off*   hands on   hands around throat   control freak   out-of-control freak

the daily grind

I could've been a contender

Your ever-changing mood swings mean that whatever vocation you devote your life to at the beginning of the month will be denounced as a waste of your existence—pointless though that is—a few days later when the Moon changes shift. Bosses like you because you work hard and your Eeyore-ish presence prevents any outbreaks of unproductive *joie de vivre* in cubicleland, but don't understand your complete inability to hit a deadline when it's standing right in front of you (you're afraid of angering the gods by trying to appear in any way in control of your gloomy little corner of the universe). You like to work longer hours than anyone else, because then you can feel really put upon and get in some quality kvetching about your lot whenever you manage to trap two or three colleagues in the elevator. You also like to have a job for which you are overqualified, so that you can feel superior and tell everybody else what to do—in a caring way, of course.

Whatever job you do, you loathe it until you leave, when you instantly come over all misty eyed and look back in fond nostalgia at what fun it was and how sad it is that all things must pass.

Cancer workstation

You chose the poky, inconvenient cubicle to ensure you always have something to whine about. No one understands that the unstructured heaps of paperwork are to confuse malign fate. The janitor learns to dust round them, but forgives you because your trashcan is pristine.

If anyone criticizes your work you instantly assume the Crab Defensive Posture (you're always halfway there anyway), clam up, hunker down into your pod, switch off your phone, and glare and snap tetchily at everyone except the guilty party. People know to creep around you for a few days until the mood swing takes effect.

Bad timing

You may be actually outside the office punctually, digit poised on the entry button, or outside the meeting room, clipboard in claw, but just can't bring yourself to go in on time; it's your way to control events without appearing to.

How employable are you?

Not all that. The mood swings (although predictable) make anything that demands consistency of approach a no-no. And your strong grip on despair and the hopeless futility of existence means you cannot, in the scheme of things, behave as if the bottom line has any true significance. However, on the Brightside, you are shoo-in for the caring professions. Of course you are—it means that you only have to deal with the sad, sick, and confused; plus you can have a good wallow in other people's misery.

Mental health day count

Once a month, plus your birthday, you simply can't get out of bed. Life's just too pointless.

Dream jobs for Cancer

So what should you do in the ideal Cancerian world of work? What would suit you best and inflict the least harm on everyone else?

Agony aunt

Vicarious suffering! Transference! You get to hand out industrial amounts of compassion and motherly advice without having to come out of your shell, and they will all love you for it.

Henry VIII

Hermit

You can grump in a wet cave all day, gloom all the time, get a free hair shirt and all the hemlock you can drink— plus it's part of the job description to be bad tempered and shun visitors.

Role model

Henry VIII (June 28, 1491). This is what all Crabs are like inside, and why you fear success. Look what you might do! Dissatisfied with your partner? People criticizing your work? Off with their heads. If only it was that simple.

office politics

secrets and more secrets

You ought to be a natural, with that inbuilt tendency to move sideways and the 500 gigabytes of storage space in your back brain for all the secrets you've been told. Many a CEO who divulged things they never told anyone else when they were mere EOs now tremble in their Gucci loafers because they know you know where the bodies are. Yet you don't use these impressive advantages (Scorpio would kill for them) because, although shrewd enough to spot middle-management shenanigans while still in development, you loathe confrontation even more than you loathe taking sides. This may be because inside your inner shell (all Cancerians have two), you are secretly convinced you are better than anybody else and ought to be Queen.

Backstabbing

No, no, no—far too confrontational; instead, you bring in deli-loads of homemade, all-butter apple pie, double-choc-choc-fudge brownies, and strawberry-cream cheesecake, and hope that killer levels of LDL cholesterol will eventually clog up your rivals' arteries.

You and the greasy pole

You wish there was no such thing as a career ladder, or that it ran horizontally, as you have a morbid fear of success because it will make you conspicuous—easy pickings for the malign yet gourmet gods who like crab mayo for lunch. It is much better to preempt disaster by sawing through the rungs yourself. Every time promotion looms, you deliberately blow the review or move to another company, where you can start again on a lower rung; you'll swallow the pay dive to avoid the stress. However, although crabs don't climb, they do cling on, and you are rarely fired.

Brown-nose index

Low. You always try to have a pleasant word for everyone because you can't bear not to be loved, so don't make any extra effort for the boss. But the boss, sensing you are not after her job, tends to be pleasant to you, which gets you an undeserved rep for graduate-level brown-nosing.

Watercooler moment

Your natural home; everybody gather around Mom for a show-and-tell session. It's always more satisfying if disaster has struck one of your brood and they need comforting.

offiçe fun

tears before bedtime

Look, someone's got to be Mom. It's a thankless task (not that you actually expect any thanks), but someone has to be the grown-up, sensible one (no, Cancer is not a party pooper, thank you, Gemini) and calm everyone down ready for home time, after Aries and Sagittarius have hyped them up into a frenzy and made them all shouty and overtired. (If you don't put that highlighter pen down this minute, you'll have someone's eye out.) That's you, Momma Jekyll, for three-quarters of the month. For the other quarter, you morph into your manic laughing-in-the-face-of-the-universe-and-dancing-on-the-edge-of-the-abyss mode, and twinkle from cube to cube, distracting everyone from their work with bad puns and snappy put-downs.

Office romance

Of course you harbor immortal longings for unsuitable partners at the office, but show it by never speaking to them and leaving the cube/atrium/washroom whenever they come in, so they think you hate them. If it does go right, you keep it secret by setting up a special e-mail address and sending coded attachments. You and another Crab could happily carry on an intense affair right up to the day you both pick up your gold watches and no one would be any the wiser.

Dress-down disasters

Bless! You think they mean it. You hate being trapped in a suit, so love showing up in your paint-stained sweat pants and college football shirt, or the tie-dye kaftan you snapped up in a thrift store on Haight-Asbury.

Office party

You dread office parties as you do any parties, so spend the evening tidying up empty glasses, replenishing nibble dishes, and generally doing the catering staff's job (they all go out back for a quick spliff). Even worse are team-bonding outings, where you might have to do role-play or karaoke or demonstrate your lack of juggling skills in front of everyone. That's why you leave and go freelance.

Your cheapest trick

You are far too occupied sweeping the area to detect any dirty tricks being played on you to have time to think up tricks of your own. And isn't life one huge cruel trick anyway? But you do enjoy the look on Virgo's face when you reveal you have reorganized their filing system to comply with yours.

teamwork

momma knows best

In any group of more than two, you switch to Automatic Nurturing Mode and start scrubbing people's cheeks, telling them they need a warmer jacket, etc. For some reason, team members resent this. You feel slighted and unappreciated (it doesn't take much) and punish people by Not Speaking To Them. They don't notice, but it makes a sham of the daily Strategy & Planning meetings. Your fear of success stops many a team initiative in its tracks (you'd rather wander the road less taken), unless there's a particularly mouthy and rebellious Aries on board. You never squeal on a colleague, because family is family, and you like that comfortable martyrish feeling when you take the blame instead—but they'll get a good telling off later.

Leader, follower, passenger, grunt

As a cardinal sign you have the leadership impulse, but not in a good way; you are either in pole position on Team Lemming (glorious, pointless sacrifice) or the charismatic leader of a suicide cult (more of the same). As a follower, you tetch quietly but constantly in the back seat, muttering about the route you would have taken. You'd feel guilty about being carried along as a passenger, but would love it down in steerage among the grunts, where you can matronize people less fortunate than yourself, who know how to be grateful for your unstoppable care.

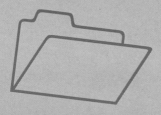

Know your enemies

Aries—the zodiac's adolescent: you can beat them by playing the Mom card.

Taurus—bring in homemade brownies to keep them in their stall and out of action.

Gemini—be careful: you're a sucker for a flattering flirt, and they will suck you dry.

Cancer—you creep up on them sideways; they creep up on you sideways. Impasse.

Leo—you're a Water sign, they're a Fire sign; use your gloom to douse their flames.

Virgo—ask maternally about their health to divert the constant steam of criticism.

Libra—a fellow cardinal, but don't rely on their loyalty if a better offer comes along.

Scorpio—watery like you, but with focus and a weapon; your shell will keep them out.

Sagittarius—tire them out by letting them scream and shout at the end of the day.

Capricorn—your opposite sign, and just as curmudgeonly as you. Avoid each other.

Aquarius—all that rebelling is just a phase; they'll get over it and settle down soon.

Pisces—you always fall for their latest sob story and let them swim all over you.

Are you talking to me?

Most of your communication is via e-mail or SMS; it's far too scary to bark out direct orders. People should know what you mean by your tone of voice and body language. If they have to ask, you sure as hell aren't going to tell them.

Worst-case scenario

From the company's POV, a team of Cancerians downgrades all performance indicators. Nothing gets done as you all contemplate the vast littleness of life; a SEAL unit of Earth signs has to be dropped in to get the ship moving again.

Lεθ

♌

July 23–August 23
Line Manager: Suŋ

Successful applicants will boast unjustified levels of self-confidence and will have completed a PhD in both Histrionics and Extreme Vanity. An egocentric worldview is essential, as is a familiarity with contempt. A talent for flouncing and sulking is also an advantage. Candidates will be expected to condescend and patronize across all industry sectors, and intolerant bossiness is a core skill. Auditions will be held in Las Vegas, and applicants should demonstrate all-around arrogance, pomposity, and bombast (and supply their own klieg lights and makeup artist). Candidates who fail are expected to stand center stage, go pale with fury, and demand to be judged by a higher authority. Positive discrimination will be shown to sycophancy addicts.

Workaholics

You are always on show, meeting and greeting; you never complain about how many weeks you have to spend traveling the world or how many five-star meals you have to eat.

Show me the money

Vulgar stuff, money: you'd prefer to be paid in gold or small countries, but as a modern monarch you'll graciously make do with a three-figure salary, and a Black card. You're worth it.

Excuses, excuses

You can't be in the office every day because of your duties as patron of the entertainment industry. If you call in sick, it will be your back that's gone, strained by supporting your crown.

comatose   laid-back   hands off   hands on   hands around throat   *control freak*   out-of-control freak

the daiLy grind

you're the boss

As long as you're the center of attention, the actual job is a smidge irrelevant. Whatever it is, you must: a) be in charge; b) be seen to be in charge. You will also expect as standard an admiring entourage of slavish acolytes (minimum three) to do the heavy work and the fawning. Now you can really start some serious ruling. Your strategy in any work situation is to sweep in, impose your authority, and to punish treasonable behavior—anyone who does not agree with your perfectly reasonable demands or old favorites from the previous monarch's reign. You can do this with a clear conscience because you are king, and anyway lions always eat the progeny of the deposed leader of the pride. It's nature's way. That's why astute employers often take you on as a hatchet person; it only costs them a big desk and an imposing title.

You may appear to be a workaholic, but you are really only good at face time; you know too well that you can be titanically lazy. Have you see what male lions do all day? Lolling on velvet divans being fed peeled grapes and watching the workforce sweat is part of the job description, isn't it?

Leo workstation

It's easy to spot the Leo workspace —it's surrounded by a moat of respectful distance. You bullied Admin into ordering you a plusher chair than anyone else, and on your desk sits your Smythson diary and the Mont Blanc but no actual work— you have people to do that.

Anyone who criticizes your work is just asking for a mauling. You are never wrong. Of course, you don't condescend to respond to anything that low on your radar, but when the upstart comes back from lunch they find they have been exiled to the satellite company in Somewhere, Iowa, where they deal solely in hog futures.

Bad timing

How could you be late? It's like saying the Sun's late. Surely nothing of any importance starts until you make an entrance? If it does, you flounce out in a hissy fit and refuse to come back for days. You have your pride, you know.

How employable are you?

Dull businesses that need to up their profile with a patina of style or a jolt of chutzpah red-carpet you. Although you like money, what you like even better is applause and sycophantic adoration in the rock-star class. (That's why you are sometimes the handsome heart surgeon working selflessly pro bono—a theater is a theater). You will always pass up an anonymous bit-part in a blue-chip company for the starring role (and the lion's share of the take) in some ramshackle out-of-town production.

Mental health day count

Low. You know only too well what happens to kings when they take their eye off the throne.

Dream jobs for Leo

So what should you do in the ideal Leo world of work? What would suit you best and inflict the least harm on everyone else?

Televangelist

Beam yourself into every home, deliver showmanship, sincerity, and loads of slap, receive the love and money of the millions, and hot-wire yourself to the Supreme Being. Praise the Lord!

Celeb

Drench yourself in hot white limelight, thrill to the roar of the crowd, feel the love of the little people! But drive everywhere in a sealed limo—you don't want body contact with the sweaty little commoners.

Role model

Napoleon Bonaparte (August 15, 1769). So he was a republican—that was just a disguise, sometimes a king in exile has to roll with the punches. Yet from a standing start as a tiny Corsican nobody, he clawed his way up to become Emperor of France. Now that's the way to start a dynasty.

Napoleon Bonaparte

office politics

down in jungle land

Kings don't get to be kings—at least not for long—if they have no political smarts or lack the will to power. It may not always look like it (as some of you can only do sledgehammer) but you are always politicking. Officially, you don't do office gossip; unofficially, you have organized a posse of sycophantic informers whose balls you have in a vise and who report to you at noon. And that vanity mirror helps you to look secretly behind you, to see who's getting close with a knife. It's second nature for you to form alliances (usually temporary) with the right kind of people, and you have never had any trouble dropping the wrong kind of people without a thought. If your allies defect, you have generations of arrogant bullying to fall back on.

Backstabbing

Gemini is on the payroll to kill off your enemies without you having to know, so that you can offer a eulogy to their family with a genuine tear in your eye; but if the entourage starts getting uppity, you like to remind them who's boss by staging a full-scale public execution.

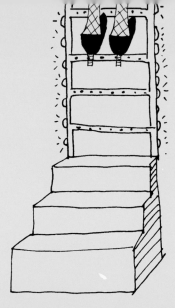

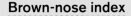

You and the greasy pole

Work your way up the hierarchy? Excuse me! Whatever your position in the office, you are already, in your eyes, the boss. It would be beneath you to scramble on the communal ladder with the common people. Darlings though they are, they smell. You expect some jostling with other Leos, of course, and maybe with the odd self-made emperor (Scorpio), but that will be on a superior royal ladder. You either marry your rivals, buy them off, or administer the killing bite just at the weak spot at back of the neck when they least expect it.

Brown-nose index

Below the radar—you only slime around other kings who have what you want (you call this statecraft). If you don't have a key to the executive washroom, you order a serf to make a duplicate. Far more important is your own Brown Nose RDA: you need to be drip-fed megadoses of flattery on the hour.

Watercooler moment

You have your own supply of mineral water, but patronize the watercooler every now and then to see what people really think of you. It's not always good.

office fun

show business

When you are in Good King mode, you easily persuade everyone to sign up for the office musical (directed by you, with you as the lead) or the interdepartmental talent contest (which you are going to win). If you are feeling particularly Marie-Antoinette, you bring in basketloads of delicious little home-built cupcakes for everyone, to show that you have the Common Touch. And you are a natural at those sincere, tear-jerking goodbye speeches when dull people, whom no one can remember, leave. However, if you're having one of your hollow-crown moments, you go into a monumental sulk, kill any office levity stone-dead, and order everyone to stop having fun and get back to scraping a living off the land—or whatever it is they do.

Office romance

You would not be taking your rank seriously if you did not seduce all the best-looking people in the office (it's called *droit de seigneur*—or *madame*). What's the point of a big corner office with a king-sized desk if you don't use it? Subtle you're not.

Floral bouquets the size of redwoods crowd the desk of the doe-eyed PR babe; the cute new boy in Accounts packs a gold-plated iPod. Your seducees know about each other, but it's a relief to have other people to share sycophancy duty.

Dress-down disasters

You've spent all week disguised as a poor but honest drudge (apart from your Agent Provocateur underwear). Now show who's boss in leopard print, gold lamé, ruffled shirt, ruby slippers, maximum bling, and a hat. Make sure the labels show.

Office party

It's always a dilemma for you, because you are torn between your insatiable need to be the center of attention and your raging snobbery. (Who are these ghastly little people?) As a trade-off you usually turn up, laugh heartily, make a crowd-pleasing speech, have a bop with the least unattractive of your colleagues, maybe even put on a funny hat, then leave discreetly in a black-windowed limo.

Your cheapest trick

As the zodiac's Drama Queen in Residence, you are convincing when you announce that the company has been subject to a reverse takeover/ is diversifying into bat guano/will be relocating to Guam. Smile inwardly as everyone reorganizes their lives, then whip off the mask and reveal it was all a jape. Sulk when you get no applause.

teamwork

it's a pride thing

Of course, you can't work without a team (your hairdresser, nutritionist, fitness coach, astrologer, aura-cleanser, florist, a couple of gophers, the little man who organizes your rider), although it sounds a bit grimily communal—you prefer the terms "retinue," "entourage," or even "pride." Your idea of teamwork is you telling everyone else what to do; you are the star player, after all. Fortunately you are never wrong, so everything always works out fine. You're off book with the humble speech you'll make when your team picks up the office Oscar. Cooperation and pulling together are not part of the deal. What are lions? Big cats. And are cats famous for their all-for-one-and-one-for-all ethic? Ever seen a team of cats pulling a sled across the Arctic waste?

Leader, follower, passenger, grunt

Do you have to ask? Leader, of course—even if there are only two of you in the company. You are an impatient follower and find it hard to disguise your lust for the crown, but smarter Lions know how to act humble while waiting for that perfect coup moment. Monumental laziness makes it easy for you to ride along as passenger, but it saps your strength and turns you into one of those wasted playboy royals. Grunt? Never: or only if you're going undercover to find out what, precisely, is rotten in your realm or to destroy the ring of dark power and mend the sword that was broken.

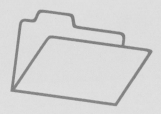

Know your enemies

Aries—sideline their ambition in style by making them chief of the Honolulu office.

Taurus—never antagonize the workers; bribe them with shiny things instead.

Gemini—*et tu*, Brute! And you thought they really did worship and adore you.

Cancer—don't listen to all the negative fretting, it will bring on your stage fright.

Leo—two topcats on one patch is never going to work; one of you will have to die.

Virgo—behead them now, before the nagging reduces you to undignified mauling.

Libra—will flatter you until are unable to stop yourself making them Vice President.

Scorpio—follow the first rule of ruling: keep your friends close, and your enemies closer.

Sagittarius—will undermine you with their "emperor's new clothes"-style comments.

Capricorn—will cancel your gorgeous office refurbishment, because it's over budget.

Aquarius—your opposite sign, republican to your royal; watch out for tumbrils.

Pisces—you don't like getting your paws wet, so why mess in these murky waters?

Are you talking to me?

Well, this is a no-brainer. Surely your commands could not be clearer. You project well, with clear, dramatic gestures. If that doesn't get the word across, there's always roaring and tail-lashing to make your intentions crystal clear.

Worst-case scenario

From the company's POV, a team of Leos means that nothing gets done while there is a vicious fight to the death for the crown. An Aries tyrant sent in to usurp power will force everyone into a temporary alliance to bring him/her down.

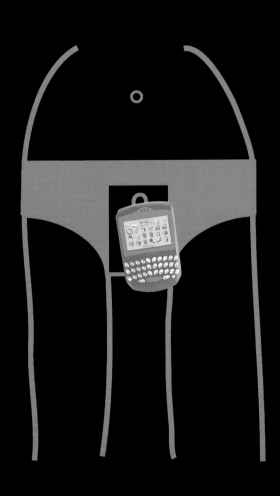

Virgo ⊙

♍

August 24–September 22
Line Manager: Mercury

This demanding post prioritizes candidates with exemplary sphincter control and a fetish for detail. Applicants will be judged on lint-picking ability, all-round pettiness, hypercritical carping skills, and hands-on pedantry, and should hold a state-accredited diploma in Knowing Best. Candidates are expected to bring their own antibacterial wipes to interview, and to clean their chair before sitting down to inform the panel that their recruiting technique does not conform to current best practice. An ability to combine a Stakhanovite work ethic with a measurable deficit in deliverables is essential. The Zodiac Corporation fully supports a policy of positive discrimination toward terminal hypochondriacs in the nonrecovery phase of OCD.

Workaholics

Five-star. Unable to switch off, you can't accept the office won't fall apart without you; they will have to pry the laptop, BlackBerry, and cellphone from your cold, dead hand.

Show me the money

It's not the money (though you won't say no)—it's the status and respect you crave. You are very proud of your ability to look neat and tidy on $3 a day and a tofu lunch pack.

Excuses, excuses

You can't bear to pass up a chance to come in and show off your textbook symptoms of the *syndrome du jour*, but like to curl up at home in private with your particular favorite: IBS.

comatose   laid-back   hands off   hands on   hands around   control   out-of-control

the daily grind

you don't want to do it like that

You love work because if it wasn't for work, you would have to talk to your family and get a life. And where else can you get to tell people how to do things properly all day long and they can't beat you up about it? Bosses love you to begin with: you are the perfect lackey, ready at a moment's notice to put in extra weekends or cancel that trip-of-a-lifetime ride on the space shuttle (you are only going because you know that space is nice and sterile) to implement the stationery directive. You love to serve somebody, because once you are running their life (you are such an organizational treasure), you have them in your power. They often realize this too late to do anything about it.

Eventually it dawns on management that you put in long hours not because you are forging ahead and taking the company with you, but because you are mired in detail. You spend at least an hour each morning color-coding your erasers. But they can't fire you; you have made yourself indispensable because you are the only one who understands the database that you set up, since you were the only one who could be bothered to read the manual.

Virgo workstation

Your station is easily identified by the grid of sticky notes containing your lists. The master List of Lists is in a top drawer of the six filing cabinets guarding the area. Your six-pack of Pledge is stowed under your desk, by the drawer full of no-fat, sugar-free oat bars and decaf pumpkin seeds.

No one ever criticizes your work more than once. Not only are you are backed up to the hilt with sources, double-checked references, and authorization from POTUS, but will switch to Withering Nitpickery Mode and highlight the statistical anomalies in their methodology, using information from e-mails they thought everyone had trashed

Bad timing

Always just before the dot, so you can set your stopwatch to timetable everybody's day. And usually slightly damp and smelling of Clorox®, because you have power-walked in and just emerged from the first of the day's antibacterial showers.

How employable are you?

Remarkably. The rest of the pod can't believe their luck when you show up, because you can be counted on to do all the dull, boring jobs— Libra soon cottons on to the scam of starting to do a job badly, just so that you can show them how to do it, then do it yourself. You are magnetized by the caring professions (rafts of the inadequate crying out for organization), but should not be let anywhere near a deadline: your killer perfectionism means that you never let a project go

Mental health day count

None. How could you not be bothered to come to work? Who would run the world?

Dream jobs for Virgo

So what should you do in the ideal Virgoan world of work? What would suit you best and inflict the least harm on everyone else?

Forensic accountant

Long days at the desk nitpicking your way through ancient records tracing ingenious patterns of creative fraudulence, made by people whose attention to detail was awesome, but can't touch yours.

Elizabeth I

Internet chatroom moderator

Mixes prudery, perversion (your very secret vice), and telling others what they should think—all in one absorbing activity. And don't you just love tracing the patterns of a thread back to its nasty little perpetrator, and outing them?

Role model

Elizabeth I of England (September 7, 1533). The Virgin Queen herself. Worked twice as hard as any king—and made sure everybody knew about it. Paid great attention to detail, and so foiled all the plots made against her, and got people to throw their best cloaks into the mud so she wouldn't have to step in the doo-doo and get dirty.

office politics

dishing the dirt

Just because you're an Earth sign doesn't mean you can't be devious when you feel like it. Let's not forget that you report to Mercury, planet of tricksiness and bitchery. Spite, sarcasm, backbiting, gossipmongering, and snitching on juniors who use the Net for non work-related purposes are second nature. Your legendary data-gathering skills mean that eventually you have the dirt on everybody. Instead of profitably leasing the data mine to Scorpio or Gemini, who would use it like a stealth bomber, you try to deploy it yourself. (No one tells Virgo how to do it.) As you simply can't stop yourself explaining the finely organized detail of your cunning plan and demonstrating your workings, your intended target spots the coup coming and calls in sick that day.

Backstabbing

Grand gestures are *so* not you. Instead, you devise an impossible work schedule and merge it with an incompatible agenda, add penalty clauses for late delivery, copy it to the boss (who you know won't look at it), then watch them squirm and writhe. That'll teach them.

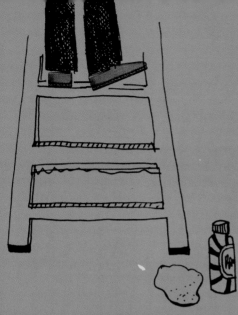

You and the greasy pole

At last: some organization in what is, quite frankly, a chaotic universe. It must have been devised by a fellow Virgo, but you can't help thinking it would be improved if every rung was clearly labeled and had a badge of status attached—and you will be sure to file a report about this. You busy yourself polishing your own rung until it gleams. You claim this makes life easier for your successor, although it actually means they slide off the minute they step on it. This makes you look perfect, and ensures there's no one riding your ass.

Brown-nose index

You come in at three, surprisingly low for one so in bed with the idea of duty. It's because you have an allergy to diplomacy, and can't stop yourself pedantically correcting the boss's grammar/punchline/pronunciation even when you are together on the podium, being beamed out on prime-time, collecting the Outstanding Performance award.

Watercooler moment

Unbeatable info-harvesting location, and a great chance to discuss the effectiveness of your new megadose vitamin enema.

office fun

what's that?

You distrust any kind of fun. Of course you do—what kind of self-respecting control freak would you be, if you didn't fear anarchy? Deep down you are scared that you might lose your grip and unleash the barely controlled hysteria that we can all see throbbing in that vein on the side of your neck. As your department's Health and Safety Rep (come on, who else would it be?), you disapprove of all practical jokes, but secretly love it when one of the Office Chair-Spinning World Series play-offs ends in a bloodbath, because then you get to say "I told you so," and be efficient with bandages and pressing on the right arterial points until the paramedics arrive—then you can tell *them* what to do. The day would not be wasted after all.

Office romance

Because you are so picky, and allergic to photocopier toner, your chances of a romance in the office are as fat as they are out in real world. However, if you work in healthcare, where there are sterilized sluice rooms and rubber gloves, the heady smell of Hibiscrub will go to your head, and anyone in a white coat will do. You are the sign most likely to out any lovers in the office: not only is it against the rules, but they didn't fill in the risk-assessment form.

Dress-down disasters

Your work clothes are organized so that you can find them in the dark, and the Coordination Rota for accessories has. been cross-checked and set for the year. And you should disrupt this meticulous garment routine for what, exactly?

Office party

This presents a challenge you can't resist, and you fret until you can take it over, sack the caterers, cancel the chocolate fountain, and stay up all night slaving over tofu sushi and carrot batons. And devise a quiz. However, as the drink is free, you are soon comatose under the table; then the boss gains popularity points by dialing the nearest pizza place. That was your plan all along, of course.

Your cheapest trick

You don't need to work at this, because your fusspot tiny-mindedness already irritates everybody to justifiable-homicide levels. But you are an absolute cinch for a wind-up yourself, and Gemini only has to retool your iCalendar for you to explode entertainingly in a self-righteous huff, like a candy-free, treat-free, fun-free piñata.

teamwork

killer driller

Although not the team leader, you are the self-appointed coach, and judge all team members against a level of perfectionism even you can't reach (although teams of psychotic plowhorses wouldn't get you to admit that). Working with you is way too irritating, so people sign up for the transfer list as soon as they get a window. So now you are a team of one which means you have to do everything, but at least you know it's being done properly and you are in control. Of course you betray anyone who is transgressing the company line—you are only doing your duty. You tell them beforehand exactly why it is their own fault, and then again afterward when they are on their way out, sobbing; but give them a free sample of your Rescue Remedy.

Leader, follower, passenger, grunt

You're not keen on being leader, because although you know you're right, in your secret dreams you fear you may not be. Follower? Yes: the chance to be the slavish Number 2, who alone knows what the Great Leader means and splits the office into easy-to-micromanage factions. A passenger you could do—lots of opportunity for complaining about the cost, service, etc. Down in grunt class you're first in line for a friendly-fire incident. Nobody likes a smart-ass.

Know your enemies

Aries—you offer detailed constructive criticism; they burn down your workstation.

Taurus—okay, they're an Earth sign too, but sitting next to all that meat makes you antsy.

Gemini—how can perfect you share a line manager (Mercury) with such a lightweight?

Cancer—you tidy their desktop and file their unstructured heaps; they get crabby.

Leo—always making grand gestures and ignoring your advice about the small print.

Virgo—how can you work with someone so OC about their health and work routine?

Libra—somehow you always do the research and they always win the Nobels.

Scorpio—give in gracelessly; you're never going to obsess to their high standard.

Sagittarius—shreds all your reports unread and corners the market in kitty litter.

Capricorn—sacks you on Christmas Eve; you can't help admiring them.

Aquarius—you file a complaint about their timekeeping; they eat your pot plant.

Pisces—your opposite sign, wet and messy where you are arid and organized.

Are you talking to me?

Hell, yeah. You info-bomb everyone, in triplicate, via speech, cellphone, landline, e-mail (with multiple attachments), SMS, hard-copy, and Fedex, but there's no talking to you. You want obedience from those with whom you communicate, not feedback.

Worst-case scenario

From the company's POV, a team of Virgos means, perversely, chaos. You all know best and will not tolerate any methodology but your own. A Scorpio slave-driver is the only way to get you to row in the same direction, although you will complain incessantly.

Taurus

Leo

Scorpio

Aquarius

Natural Born Middle Management

As you will have seen in the minutes of the first break (*page 54*) and the notes about qualities, elements, and opposites (*page 6*), these sections are about quality control. This one is the lunch break from the daily grind, but there is no reason why it can't be a working lunch, so now we are going to look at the fixed quality, the one that, in theory, produces the Natural Born Middle Manager.

Fixed signs never shrink from telling it like it is, and don't hide their nature behind a Latin uptitle (cardinal) or therapy-speak for fickle (mutable). They are called fixed signs because that's what they are. They come along after the devastation of Hurricane Cardinal and clear up the mess, try to implement whatever barking commands the cardinal issued, and do a bit of discreet burning and looting if they think they can get away with it.

This doesn't mean that everybody in middle management is a fixed sign, but it does mean that everybody who is a fixed sign itches to impose executive control in some manner.

Taurus fixed earth

slow hand

Taurus is the first fixed sign, and it's a good thing they don't have too much imagination because they have to clean up after Aries, which could leave feebler signs claiming compensation for PTSD.

There is no rushing the Taurus middle manager, so fast-moving, savvy, 21st-century, thrusting-type enterprises that work on the wing-and-a-prayer principle should not recruit. The Taurus management style is straightforward: establish a routine (one that suits them), plow on regardless of results (good or bad), and don't mess with flexibility of any kind, because that just breeds discontent in the workforce.

Mission statement

To methodically plod as slowly as possible, commensurate with acceptable levels of forward motion.

Taurus middle managers

Saddam Hussein
Karl Marx
Sigmund Freud
Vladimir Ilych Lenin

Earth

Taurus is an Earth sign, Earth is the element of practical materialism, and fixed Earth means territory. So a Taurus middle manager's workspace, daily routine, operating system, and rung position are always vigorously defended, even if they don't wake up for anything else much, other than lunch.

Leo fixed fire

make mine a royale

Leo is the second fixed sign, and it is their job to remotivate the workforce after the paralyzing gloom bought on by Cancer's efforts to dominate through emotional blackmail. Leo does this by bashing on the bling, putting on a performance, and making 'em laugh— although not always intentionally.

The Leo middle-management style is always from the top down (none of this collective consensus nonsense) and a bit tetchy and theatrical; they are itching to be king/queen and impose their rule on everyone forever, and get edgy having to act a bit humble while waiting for their chance to snatch the crown.

Fire
Leo is a Fire sign, Fire is the element of irretrievable action, and fixed Fire is the crackling roar of a burning building. If a Leo middle manager does not get the praise and promotion they so richly deserve, they will not hesitate to throw everyone on the funeral pyre of their hopes and go out in a blaze of glory.

Mission statement

To strive on a daily basis to make Leo look as great as possible.

Leo middle managers

Fidel Castro
Benito Mussolini
Mick Jagger
Madonna

Scorpio fixed water

look into my eyes

Scorpio is the third fixed sign, and the disciplinarian who has to follow up Libra's hands-off idea of leadership. It's a freezing cold shower after you've spent too long in a warm bath of honey and rose petals, and a useful way to cull weaklings. That which does not kill you makes you stronger.

No one actually sees Scorpio middle management come in, but the air crackles and suddenly there they are and productivity levels experience peak flow. The Scorpio management style bypasses rational thought and goes directly for control of the soul. Once you've got that, there are no problems with deadlines.

Water

Scorpio is a Water sign, Water is the element of emotion and sensation, and fixed Water is a deep, tideless lake with things lurking at the bottom of it. Scorpio middle management uses the workforce fear of what may surface if they don't do as they're told, to make them do as they're told.

Mission statement

Committed to total control of everything, all the time.

Scorpio middle managers

Bill Gates
Pablo Picasso
Albert Camus
Marie Antoinette

Aquarius fixed air

different strokes

Aquarius is the fourth fixed sign, tasked with incentivizing the shriveled souls left behind after Capricorn's reign of terror. The Aquarius middle manager comes at this from a strange angle, releasing all Capricorn prisoners into the wild, then taking notes on how they cope with freedom (well, relative freedom) and making slight recalibrations.

The Aquarian style of control is strictly hands-off—more of a Jedi Mind Trick than the application of a real-world system. It does not suit all workplaces and Strictly Corporate it ain't, but HR should know that Aquarius is not going to change to suit anyone else.

Mission statement

To offer new solutions to old problems and see what happens when they don't work.

Aquarius middle managers

James Dean
Virginia Woolf
Yoko Ono
James Joyce

Air

Aquarius is an Air sign, Air is the element of intellect and communication, and fixed Air means fixed opinions; in Aquarius's world, this may well mean fixed at a compass point unrecognized by the rest of us, but no Aquarian is going to shift from their entrenched position of system-bucking individualism.

Libra

September 23–October 23
Line Manager: Venus

As this is a hands-off position, high-caliber indolence, insincerity, and inconsistency are essential. Complete lack of depth is an advantage, and style will be prioritized over substance. Applicants must be familiar with all systems of Schmooze Control, and be flattery-competent in their native language plus three others, including braille. Candidates who fail to seduce the majority of the interviewing panel within the first three minutes will be disqualified. All major credit cards must be maxed out, and successful applicants should be unable to demonstrate how they achieved these results. Expenses are commensurate with current retail trends, but candidates must supply their own whim of iron.
The position is not open to executive-decision makers.

Workaholics

You may look the part at the workstation (although you are surfing the Net for your next vacation, online dating, or looking for vintage on eBay), but it's out of office, out of mind for you.

Show me the money

You have a firm grip on what you won't get out of bed for, and can negotiate a pay rise before you've even started, plus a company credit card and perks for when you have been extraspecially lovely.

Excuses, excuses

On bad hair days, or if you've broken a nail, you call in with one of your headaches, caused by the strain on your kidney after the previous night's champagne-fest with one of your sugar daddies.

comatose   laid-back   hands off   hands on   hands around throat   control freak   out-of-control freak

the daily grind

a four-letter word

Here's the problem: you are allergic to the word "job," but adore luxury and lovely things. You want it all, now, (and some to squirrel away for later), but can't understand why you have to actually do anything to get it. It's not laziness, it's discrimination and style. Why can't you be paid just to be an ornament to society? If you haven't inherited or married money, there's always the gigolo/gigolette option: okay while you're young and fit, but not very secure—and you love security. The only way forward is to find work that suits your style: it doesn't much matter what, as long as it doesn't involve actual work, ugly clothes, or unpleasant locations too many blocks from Bloomingdale's.

On the days you do show up, you get on rather well, because inside that velvet glove is a beautifully manicured iron fist. You may appear soft and easy, but all that fluttering of your long Hollywood eyelashes is so that rivals don't get a chance to look into your cold, calculating eyes. You were teacher's pet at school, and it doesn't take you more than a toss of your curls to be the boss's pet at work. You can't see what's wrong with the casting-couch system.

Libra workstation

Your workstation is beautifully free from unsightly workclutter and positively throbs with harmonious chi. It is, quite coincidentally, within whispering distance of the boss's office, because that's where the light falls most beautifully on your profile when you look up from your day bed.

Most colleagues are so bedazzled by your loveliness that they would never dream of criticizing your work. Surely it's impressive enough that you can do anything at all? But if one does, your eyes brim with crystal tears, your lips quiver, and you ask for help; they feel so heelish that they do the work for you.

Bad timing

Always late, either because you had to wait for delivery of your Kate Spade tote or stop off for new underwear, but always immaculate and just in time for the killer meeting for which your assistant has done all the research.

How employable are you?

An active connoisseur of leisure like you should not be made to work. The economy may be better off if you stick to shopping. You may refuse to sweat, but you do ooze charm, so you are an asset to any dream factory (the movie industry, advertising, PR, fashion) or anywhere that needs more spin than Gemini can handle. You'd be great as the front-of-house face for companies that do grim things no one wants to talk about: Legirons 'R' Us, maybe, or Toxic Waste International.

Mental health day count

High. Rarely a day goes past when you don't feel just that little bit too fragile before noon.

Dream jobs for Libra

So what should you do in the ideal Libran world of work? What would suit you best and inflict the least harm on everyone else?

Fashion maven

Achingly chic in head-to-toe black, you dictate what everyone else should wear, and get to make people who are richer and more successful than you look ugly and foolish, ha-ha. Plus you get free stuff.

Richard III

Spin doctor

It's the old straw-into-gold boffo. Take any piece of info—especially the dull or damaging kind—and spin it into a web of silken verbiage until it gleams. You can do this in your sleep, which is your work mode of choice, after all.

Role model

Richard III (October 2, 1452). Despite a fearsome rep as a child murderer, he has an international society dedicated to making him look better than he actually was. Smooth-talking charm that still works after half a millennium in the grave. Top stuff.

office politics

charm offensive

Forget about all that dreary work (you've delegated that back on page 94 anyway), this is what you are really here for: gliding effortlessly across the Lake Treachery that is office politics, while paddling like fury underneath. Impeccable manners are a perfect disguise, especially to office thugs who haven't got any and don't understand that diplomacy is war conducted by other means: that is, without the shouting and noise. In any standoff you never take sides (you let people think this is because of your famous Indecisive Dither Syndrome), because you intend to be with the winners when it's all over and don't want to declare early out of anything like principle or loyalty. If there was a workplace fence, you'd have a recliner on it.

Backstabbing

It all sounds far too sweaty for you, and what about the blood spatter? Whatever Martha says, it will never come out. Much better to marinate your enemies in honey and then sit back and sympathize soothingly while the ants make a meal of them.

You and the greasy pole

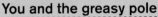

A ladder! For you? Ooh, how deliciously vertical. Of course, you're more used to a couch, but you'll give it your best shot. Oh dear, you don't think you'll be able to manage it on your own; maybe the CEO would give you a leg-up, just onto the first rung? You would be *so* grateful. Maybe you should just slip off these hot shoes to get a better grip. How kind of the VP to pull you onto that last rung. Aw, you guys! Look, we're at the top already—wasn't that quick. And, really, it didn't seem difficult at all.

Brown-nose index

Off the scale. How can you breathe and talk with your nose buried that deep in the collective bossly tuchus? A couple of signs can see through the smarmscreen to the grasping manipulator beyond, but you just smile beautifully and plot a new angle of approach to them, one that makes you look charmingly Amish and plain-speaking.

Watercooler moment

Your ideal basking ground—everybody has to come past it at some point, and you'll be waiting to charm them into trouble.

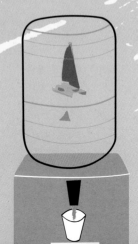

office fun

distractor fan

Poise and balance are what Libra is about, so you curl your lovely pouty lip at sweaty games or jock-style pranking. On the other hand, you're up for anything that distracts from dull old work, because behind the smooth exterior you are insatiably restless and antsy. It's all done with your signature manipulation style; it takes you no time to charm Sagittarius into playing their hilarious elevator game, so that the circuits frazzle and that cute engineer has to come and fix them—again. If the Prada sale is on, you dare Aries to turn the sprinklers on using only a rubber band and a binder clip. While the system is reset, you'll all get three hours off. Everyone below boss class will love you even more; if there are repercussions, they won't stick to you.

Office romance

You flirt with everybody in the office, or just passing the office, regardless of gender, age, status, or even species. You were, after all, trained by Venus. Of course, you get lucky (saturation bombing always hits somebody), but you particularly favor the plain or dorky because: a) they complement your charm and beauty so well; b) they usually possess the key to somewhere important, or are so grateful they willingly blow three months' salary on that Bulgari watch you really, really need

Dress-down disasters

Dress down? What can they mean? You always dress to kill (you can look good in a garbage operative's vest, with the right accessories). So, of course, you'd love to show all the grubby little people how to dress, but you don't do Fridays.

Office party

This is where you really go to work. Want a salary hike? Work the room, liberate a magnum of Cristal, stick two straws in it, corral the boss, and lure him/her out to the stretch limo you have hired on expenses. Drive off into the night to negotiate with their affections. At team-bonding weekends, stay at base looking cute in your Juicy Couture, ready to admire the boss's croc-wrestling skills.

Your cheapest trick

You are so used to winding everyone around your pinkie that trickery is almost no fun anymore. One you most enjoy is giving the office scarecrow a makeover—recommending colors and styles that are, oh, almost two seasons old! Aren't you the clever one? The downside is you're the only one who finds it funny.

teamwork

all for one

Naive team leaders want to get you signed up a.s.a.p., seeing you as the oil on the wheels driving them to success. You *are* nice to look at and get on *so* well with everybody. Invariably elected team rep (*Moi?* You are too kind!) because you negotiate with the boss class so well; it's only when you're on the board and they're in the parking lot with their personal possessions in a box that your team realizes what has happened. Even then, they are sure you did your best. (You did.) You only ever drop colleagues in it when you're sure they can no longer play a useful part in your Career Management Plan—usually by telling the boss you are so glad that X is out of rehab again, and haven't they done well, despite everything.

Leader, follower, passenger, grunt

Not leader: that would mean making a decision, and how can you know it would be the right one (for you) until you've seen someone else fail? Follower? Better, but you prefer a nice ambivalent term, like ambassador, to talk your way out of any blame. You are one of nature's passengers. Why work when you can watch someone else's muscles ripple agreeably while you sip martinis? And someone who looks as cute as you do in coveralls is not going to stay a grunt for long; the boss will soon fish you out of the pool.

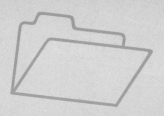

Know your enemies

Aries—your opposite sign, so very easy to manipulate into backing up your schemes.

Taurus—shares your line manager (Venus), so why shouldn't they share their bonus?

Gemini—they can charm and flirt, but you own the casting couch and the cathouse.

Cancer—easy to flatter, and will roll over and let you butter their soft underbelly.

Leo—schmoozing 101: look sincere, tell them they're wonderful, get a salary hike.

Virgo—it would be cruel not to let them do all the work—it's all they have, after all.

Libra—what happens when two airheads collide? A vacuum or a black hole is what.

Scorpio—take control by turning down their lust offers; you're the only sign that can.

Sagittarius—your diplomatic skills are wasted here; just shout or yank the reins.

Capricorn—cuts the hospitality budget to ribbons that your charm can't restitch.

Aquarius—avoid; far too chilly to be around, and you can't bear to be uncomfortable.

Pisces—almost as good as you at doing nothing, but without the style or panache.

Are you talking to me?

Everybody thinks they know what you mean as you smile charmingly, look sincerely into their eyes, and tell them all you think they need to know. If that doesn't get them, your body language will. And how useful is feedback? All the ammo you need, for free.

Worst-case scenario

From the company's POV, a team of Librans brings everything to a graceful standstill while you wait for one another to make the first move. A Sagittarian will get the team going again, even if it's just to get away from the noise.

Scorpio

♏

October 24–November 21

Line Manager: Pluto

Minimum requirements for this position are a Masters in Manipulation with Menaces and an all-black wardrobe. Candidates will be motivated by a very high lust drive and will demonstrate advanced skills in the fields of jealousy, possessiveness, and revenge. A high Intense Brooding Capacity is essential, and applicants with an uncontrollable mania for control will take priority. Anything lower than an insane level of competitiveness is unacceptable. Successful candidates must be able to frighten the selection panel into giving them the job before the interview has started and answer any questions with contemptuous silence. Outbreaks of psychotic bad temper and an ability to self-destruct at will are regarded as core strengths.

Workaholics

Extreme. Either 26 hours a day at the office seven days a week and no home life, or 26 hours a day seven days a week in the dumpster with a bucket of crystal meth and no home life.

Show me the money

Fee negotiations are always successful, but, really, there's not enough wealth in the world to fill you up, so you're just as likely to take the abject-poverty route to show how disciplined you are.

Excuses, excuses

You never call in sick—that would show weakness, a gift to your enemies. You just don't show, and we're all too scared to ask why. You're often unavoidably detained at the STD clinic.

comatose   laid-back   hands-off   hands-on   hands-around   control   out-of-control

the daily grind

in control

Nothing and nobody gets in the way of your career path. When not actually working, you are retrieving staff e-mails, shredding secret papers, changing the password on your hard drive to confuse enemy hackers, and devising more efficient ways of making money. It's so much easier now that you can access everything from your power laptop, so that wherever you are, you are in control.

Scorpio workstation

The immaculate Scorpio desk is clear except for your nine black pens lined up precisely against your matt black laptop—and maybe a voodoo doll hanging from your desk lamp. Surgery could be done on your desk, and frequently is. No one knows about your drawer full of cake.

It's not as if it's difficult: act polite, dress immaculately, stay on top of the detail, and you can do anything you like, because other people are lazy, greedy, weak, and deserve exploitation. You keep your ears open and your eyes down (so rivals cannot see your power glare until you want them to), troll the database for useful contacts, then set up an evil empire of your own. Perversely, when you have trashed the opposition and your empire is at its glorious height, you like to destroy it, partly to show how hard you are, but mostly because you're cosmically bored. An alternative Scorpio strategy is to drift into a career of drinking and debauchery—to which, it must be said, you bring all the focus, determination, and willpower that you do to any enterprise.

Only those with a death wish criticize your work. It all goes very quiet, and those who are attached to their intestines start backing silently out of the danger zone. You say nothing, but laser through your critic's front brain to reach the cowering inadequate beyond, then nuke their psyche.

Bad timing

At least two hours ahead of anyone else (you slept under your desk, or not at all) so that you can intimidate them when they come in; or deep undercover (allegedly) and out of the office for months, but still getting paid.

How employable are you?

Not at all. Ruthless but cowardly bosses who hire you as the office Dobermann soon regret it when you turn on them. Your skill set is strictly narrowband, although if there's an opening for Grand Inquisitor or dominatrix you're the one they call. Self-employment is the Only Way: you have to be able to respect the boss, after all. As an employer, you are highly successful, because you can get maximum output for minimum wage without even picking up your whip.

Mental health day count

Only if it's midweek and you're having one of your motel days with the help.

Dream jobs for Scorpio

So what should you do in the ideal Scorpio world of work? What would suit you best and inflict the least harm on everyone else?

City analyst

Get paid obscene amounts of money to play with other people's obscene amounts of money, second-guessing trends and setting up slick moves to trash the competition and earn you even more obscene amounts of money.

Professional assassin

You spurn the bread-and-butter gangland contracts for the edgy intrigue, secrecy, and destabilizing political fallout that comes with top-class, globally significant, grassy-knoll-style eliminations.
Much better paid.

Role model

Niccolò Machiavelli (May 3, 1469). Father of modern political theory and author of *The Prince* (1513), the ruthless manager's guide to raw political power. And yes, he's Taurus, your opposite sign: how typically perverse and misdirectional of you.

Niccolò Machiavelli

office politics

scare tactics

In politics (even the office kind), reputation is all, and your carefully established hardcore reputation means you don't have to do much to make things go your way —if everybody is already scared witless, they'll do your work for you. You find this method of control very energy efficient (you hate waste), because you only have to disembowel a few of the workforce to make the others understand how things are going to be. If there is insurgency, your weapons of choice are manipulation and mind gaming. Knowledge is power, and you poke and interrogate until you've found out all the shameful little secrets and vulnerable weak points and exactly what pushes our buttons. Then we know that you know, and you can do what you like with us.

Backstabbing

Yes, yes, stiletto through the eye at dead of night on a dank canal side, and all that; but what you really like is keeping your victims conscious long enough to flay them alive, so that you can discuss their shortcomings with them and teach valuable lessons about the nature of betrayal.

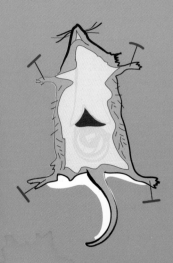

You and the greasy pole

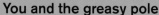

It is very easy to shimmy up the corporate ladder—be keen, polite, alert, carry no baggage, push the weak off, booby-trap the rungs as you go. Irritatingly, when you get to the top you find by some oversight (made when you were less experienced, and for which you will punish yourself remorselessly when you have a free evening) that you still don't control the ladder. Why not buy your own and make your way up it with the same ruthless efficiency? If that doesn't feel controlling enough, buy several more and go up them all at once.

Brown-nose index

You can brown-nose silkily if you want to, of course you can, it's the first module in Political Power 101, but why bother when you can get everyone to do exactly what you want just by looking at them? This does not work on other Scorpios—you just have to fight to the death. Bring it on.

Watercooler moment

The flock scatters when you stealth your way to the watercooler, because even you can't control relic atavistic behavior like survival instinct.

office fun

no laughing matter

You do not want to be popular, you want to be feared and respected, and that is not going to happen if you come on as the proprietor of Jollity Farm. So no whoopee cushions or office karaoke for you; pods full of nose-to-screen industry is what you want to see, not Gemini running Buzzword Bingo sessions. Fortunately you can nip any office merriness in the bud with just one look. You can't resist a little light torture though, reducing the office grump to a heap with a snicker-snack of your lacerating tongue. The rest of the team, fearful for their own skins, applaud sycophantically. You despise them. When you want a bit of light relief, you access the Internet porn stash that you put in the IT chief's name.

Office romance

The only thing that sidetracks you from your plans for ultimate power is sex. And because the office is where you spend most of the time, you have to recruit your lust slaves (gender is not an issue) from the podpool. Regardless of your company status, you're the one who makes the doors to the executive washroom cubicles rattle and groan—and that's just when you're on your own. The downside is that you surge back from any encounter with all batteries rejuiced and your ferocious willpower on max.

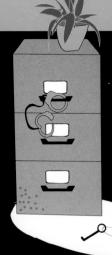

Dress-down disasters

You invented dress-down as a spiteful ruse to put your enemies off their guard. How can they oppose your new plans (cunningly introduced on a Friday) with any authority when they're dressed in surfer shorts, a Hawaiian shirt, and a Knicks cap? You wear immaculate black at all times.

Office party

Like a sinister Venetian masked ball, this is just another arena for your power games, a great opportunity to study the workforce's weaknesses so you can use them to your advantage. You lay on a gourmet buffet and free bar, but drink only water imported from a pinprick volcanic island in the Pacific and nibble at a small dish of high-protein locust, just to make everyone else feel gross.

Your cheapest trick

Merry pranks are not you, because they require a lightness of touch that you just can't manage. Plus they would ruin the whole evil-eyed control thing. It would be a bit like Lord Voldemort trying to play Santa. And no one ever dares mess with you, because your revenge is always devastating and endless.

teamwork

fixed penalties

You prefer to work alone, because carrying other people is tedious. If there's enough money in it, you will work in a team, but only if you can be leader. It's a piece of cake: you know that a tiny investment—an unexpected kindness that didn't cost you anything—yields a big payback in loyalty. When people are feeling grateful, they are weak, and that's when you weld your unit together, using abject fear as the bond. Regular culling, iron discipline, and an inflexible adherence to your way (you are a fixed sign after all) keep them up to scratch. You never turn anyone in or tell them you know what they did, because it's more punishing to let them sweat, wondering whether you do know and what you are going to do about it.

Leader, follower, passenger, grunt

Not really leader, more like Supreme Being, because people follow you whether you want them to or not, although you despise them for being so easily led. You'll only be a follower if it is more politically sound to be the invisible adviser to a puppet leader (usually Libra), but despise them for letting themselves be used. When in dumpster mode, you'll allow others to carry you as a passenger in return for your searing insights into the human condition, but despise them for being so slavish. You last three months as a grunt, through sheer willpower.

Know your enemies

Aries—control them by ordering them not to do whatever it is you want them to do.

Taurus—your embarrassingly uncool opposite sign; manipulate them with cake.

Gemini—show them your copy of their entry in the Criminal Records Bureau.

Cancer—don't waste valuable time breaking your sting on their hard shell.

Leo—ideal puppet material; let them have the crown, but keep control for yourself.

Virgo—manage them by threatening to withdraw their database-access privileges.

Libra—send them on a team-bonding cross-country run to break their spirit (and nails).

Scorpio—try a boardroom glare-out; if it goes to stalemate, quit or fight to the death.

Sagittarius—don't waste energy controlling them, they'll self-combust all by themselves.

Capricorn—challenge them to a bout of Competitive Budget Squeezing, and win.

Aquarius—act ultra-conventional; they will waste their energies trying to shock you.

Pisces—uncontrollable; fire instantly before they undermine your authority.

Are you talking to me?

You tell people what to do. They do it. Your commands could not be clearer. Your henchmen take care of any feedback that isn't either total obedience or at least total agreement with your vision. Consensus or compromise is not in the vocabulary.

Worst-case scenario

From the company's POV, a team of Scorpios means an unproductive *Reservoir Dogs*-style standoff. No one is foolhardy enough to step in. The solution is to leave you glaring implacably at each other and start a new company on another continent.

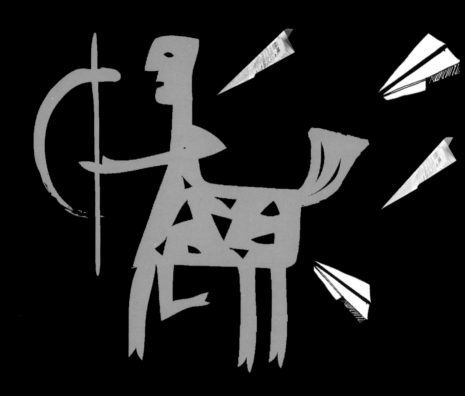

Sagittarius

November 22–December 21
Line Manager: Jupiter

The minimum qualification for this position is a high-school diploma in Hooligan Studies with Oafish Insensibility, but applicants who can demonstrate serious commitment to high-decibel impatience and insane recklessness will be at an advantage. Monumental tactlessness is a core skill, and an addiction to pointless risk is essential. Candidates will be expected to skateboard into the interview room—preferably through a closed window and on the wrong day—insult everyone, and prove that they bet their grandmother's wheelchair on whether they would get the job. This position is always oversubscribed, so successful applicants will be selected via a Russian-roulette session (revolvers supplied). Subtlety, finesse, and sensitivity are discouraged.

Workaholics

More like binge-working; either you are moonlighting for six separate companies, so take your work to your other work, or on a volcano-hopping sabbatical to give the rest of the office a rest.

Show me the money

You always ask to be paid in cash (you love the smell of burning holes in your pocket in the morning), because they won't take your scorched plastic down at the track or the mall.

Excuses, excuses

The local ER gives you frequent-flier miles, but a little thing like a shattered femur won't stop you showing up—not when you can vault in on your new turbo crutches.

| comatose | laid-back | hands off | hands on | hands around throat | control freak | out-of-contr freak |

the daily grind

risky business

On the Brightside, you should be every employer's dream: a combination of physical stamina (your inner horse) and pin-sharp, focused intelligence (your inner archer). On the Darkside , however, this just means that you are an armed animal with opposable thumbs, an unstoppable agent of chaos. To begin with, employers are blown over by what they see as your get-up-and-go, can-do,

gung-ho attitude; but then they don't usually have to share office space with you and your relentless pranks, unhilarious jokes, and tedious hoax e-mails. If the seconds begin to drag, you organize paperclip racing, inter-departmental chair-spinning contests, or trashcan infernos (you bet on whose burns longest before the sprinklers go on and the whole office closes down).

No one employs you for long, because after a while their insurance company tells them not to. But you don't care if you're canned. You much prefer being freelance (a masterless knight with a lance for hire), because you get to roam the world. The black marketeers adore you because you always lose the paperwork and don't give a rat's ass for health-and-safety regulations.

It's unlikely that you will still be there to cop any blame if anyone criticizes your work. As the zodiac's temp, you specialize in parachuting into a mission that needs help, messing it up even further, then galloping off. And if you *are* still there, you argue right back, accompanying fine philosophical insight with fine high-kicking hooves.

Bad timing

Routine just makes you cranky. So you're either already at your desk because you worked an all-nighter (great—free pizzas and milkshakes at midnight!) or five hours late because an accident (inadvertently caused by you) snarled up the entire grid.

How employable are you?

Erratically. No one could say that you are lazy: you'll do anything, anywhere, but not for long. You like to run three or four jobs at once—it doesn't matter much what kind, as long as they don't involve too much sitting down. Bike courier by day, mixologist in the evening, skydive instructor during weekends, that sort of thing. They're all located as far away from each other as possible, so you can get your fix from rollerblading, speed scooting, or subway surfing between offices.

Mental health day count

Low. You are a stranger to angst, insecurity, or self-doubt. When you don't show, it's because you're having more fun somewhere else.

Dream jobs for Sagittarius

So what should you do in the ideal Sagittarian world of work? What would suit you best and inflict the least harm on everyone else?

Stunt artist

Hang one-handed from an assault chopper. Drive high-performance cars into brick walls. Crash through plate-glass windows. Dowse yourself in gas and throw a match. And get paid for it!

Mercenary

When covert government agencies want a diehard danger-lover ready to slash through hostile terrain, live on dung beetles and recycled body fluids, then kill complete strangers in a strange land, who do you think they're gonna call?

Billy the Kid

Role model

Billy the Kid (November 23, 1859). William Bonney (actually Henry McCarty), the gunslinging cowboy from New York City. He shot and killed at least nine men (he claimed 21), and was allegedly shot down when he was young and pretty and 21, but probably ran away to Mexico and lived a whole other life.

office politics

horse sense

You have a fast flickering mind and nimble feet, so in theory office politics should be nothing more than a lively ride—but politically you are a klutz. This means you are always treading on people's toes, stumbling over buried bodies, and shouting about it, or rushing in headlong where even other fools fear to tread. Tacticians soon learn to avoid co-opting you onto their side, because you blab any secrets you are told to the next person who comes along (the very devious use you as a disinformation tool). Every now and then you accidentally succeed because Plain Speaking (a.k.a. tactless mouthing off) has its political flavor-of-the-month moment. Everyone admires your Candide approach, and Scorpio is impressed that you can keep up the act for so long.

Backstabbing

Where's the adrenaline rush in that? You're the only zodiac sign with your own weapon, and it's much more fun to ambush your enemies and let fly your arrows of spite. By the time they know what's hit them, you've packed up your quiver and galloped off to better things.

You and the greasy pole

You don't care which direction you move in—up or down—as long as you're in motion. With you snorting impatiently down their necks, meeker souls on the next rung either move on or jump; but honestly, you've only pushed one or two off, and they were accidents. Once you've cantered up and down a few career ladders, breaking the odd rung or five on the way, you are bored and trigger happy. Why not macramé your own Career Scramble Net? This offers lots of different and challenging routes to the top, a great workout—plus you might fall off. What could be more fun?

Brown-nose index

It's not just that you don't do oil and schmooze—you actively go the other way. Just as Libra is cooing over the boss's new Prada, you canter by and point out that she must have been sluicing down the carbs since she bought it. The killer is you're not bitching, just telling it like it is.

Watercooler moment

If management have any dirty information they want to give the workforce, they tell you, because you can't resist telling everyone else while you're riding the waves.

office fun

bang bang

There's nothing you won't do to entertain your workmates, because your real boss is Jupiter, the Jolly Red Giant, the bouncy planet that loves to party. Johnny Knoxville is your guru. You're the one who jams the Intranet with hilarious clips of what happens when you mix Mentos® and diet soda; the office extreme-sports coordinator (chair rowing, filing-cabinet free-running, stair surfing); the one who misdirects the major Japanese client to the janitor's closet instead of the boardroom (snigger!). If the day is slow, you dare us to dare you to do something that's so—like—crazee (rappel nude down the elevator cables, staple the boss's tie to his shirt, walk into your six-monthly review on your hands). Only elephant tranquilizers will stop you.

Office romance

As long as a coworker has a pulse, you will come on to them, but anyone expecting more than wham-bam-thank-you-ma'am should put their heart in the shredder now to save pain later. It's all just adventure and exercise to you, because you did your basic training at the Jupiter Agency, a wholly owned subsidiary of Zeus, Inc. The organization's founder spent his days manifesting to nymphs, maidens, and youths in unlikely places, when he should have been analyzing the bottom line

Dress-down disasters

The happy day sees you in your Nike Frees and performance Lycra®/wetsuit and havanas/camos and combat boots, ready to bungee jump off the roof at the end of your shift. Or you come dressed exactly as the boss, for a laugh.

Office party

As the Designated Bubbly Personality at any party, you are guaranteed to blow any chance of promotion by getting sh*t-faced and throwing up over the boss's partner. You are also the indefatigable organizer of those bonding weekends when you yomp around a muddy plain at dawn with the Accounts Department reenacting Gulf I. You don't care if no one else signs up—more ammo for you.

Your cheapest trick

What to choose? Tripping the fire alarm when everyone's working to a killer deadline? Recalibrating everyone's chairs in the night so that they look like first graders in the morning? Overdubbing the company voicemail greeting with Homer Simpson outtakes? Spiking the lattes with chili powder?

teamwork

brace! brace!

As far as your Inner Horse is concerned, you are the perfect teammate: galloping with the herd and pitching in to pull the corporate chariot across the winning line is what you do best. It's your Outer Human that's the liability—all that hyperkeen bounce-backability that got you the job in the first place ends in mutiny, chaos, and extra Band-Aids® down at the workface. Naive managers who put you in a team of cautious plodders hoping for a hi-NRG boost have only themselves to blame when you cut so many corners that the project falls to pieces, usually in front of the VP and the Money. You never give anybody up, except through sheer incompetence and your big mouth, but are regularly voted Coworker Most Likely to be Informed On by others.

Leader, follower, passenger, grunt

Cheerleader maybe, but even then you can't be relied on to turn up for practice; you'll do your own thing on the night! You love to run with the crowd as a follower, but only over a short course, and you need oversized blinkers and a carrot nailed to your forehead to stop you bolting to pastures new. And you're far too frisky to be a passenger without some serious meds. Grunthood annoys you so much you stampede the whole department into confusion.

Know your enemies

Aries—arm-wrestle them in the parking lot to establish who's on top for the day.

Taurus—will make you plod along in their rut by hiding your oats until the job's done.

Gemini—your opposite sign but smarter, so will always leave you with the smoking gun.

Cancer—they order time-out on the Naughty Step; you plan the next prank.

Leo—a brother Fire sign, so respect them, but not when they get pompous on you.

Virgo—always ready to take offense, so why not dish it out? You hate to disappoint.

Libra—bolt; they'll use velvet reins and caviar mash to turn you into a workhorse.

Scorpio—they'll try to ride you with their whip; throw them at the first bend.

Sagittarius—lay bets to see who can drive Capricorn into a murderous rage first.

Capricorn—a joy to annoy: a natural target for your whoopee cushion and joke turd.

Aquarius—this is a bit of a no-horse race, because you do slapstick and they do alt.com.

Pisces—will blame you when they mess up; so drink their hooch drawer dry in revenge.

Are you talking to me?

Too much information: unmoderated stream-of-consciousness scrawled on the back of envelopes, multiple contradictory e-mails, or instructions shouted into your cellphone as you dash off. You never stand still long enough to deal with feedback.

Worst-case scenario

From the company's POV, a team of Sagittarians either means nothing gets done or the system goes into freefall as you try to drive the project in all directions at once. A Taurus team might be able to broadside you to a stop.

Gemini

Virgo

Sagittarius

Pisces

Natural Born Slackers

As you will have seen in the minutes of the first two breaks (*pages 54 and 96*) and the notes about qualities, elements, and opposites (*page 6*), these sections are about the qualities (or lack thereof) demonstrated by the different signs. This is our last break before the end of the book, so let's get in some quality time-wasting by looking at just how hard the zodiac's Natural Born Slackers work in their various ways to undermine order, reinstate chaos, and generally establish the preconditions for a tyrant-style takeover by the cardinal signs who come after them. Then perhaps we can slide off a bit early, because everyone will have forgotten we went to the bathroom.

We're talking about the mutable signs, inevitably last in the quality sequence. Mutable means changeable (that's in its least-bad scenario), so these are the signs that—through incompetence, insolence, and general lack of moral fiber—undo all the systems that the previous fixed signs have put in place.

This doesn't mean that every slacker is a mutable sign, but that every mutable sign looks for ways to do the least, while appearing to do the most.

Gemini Mutable Air

talk the talk

Gemini is the first mutable sign, and a role model for all the others. It requires a master craftsperson to destabilize a Taurus-trained workforce, and Gemini is that crafty. No one knew they were discontented until Gemini pointed it out, twinkling about like a grasshopper in an ant colony. Everybody stops work and starts to party, until Big Momma Cancer hears the noise and comes in hard to send everyone to their rooms.

The Gemini slacker style is to look as if you are having big fun doing nothing; when nonslacker signs try it they fail, because they don't download other people's hard work first, as an alibi.

Gemini slackers

Marquis de Sade
Bob Dylan
Marilyn Monroe
Clint Eastwood

Mission statement

To entertainingly fool most of the people for the time it takes to get a new job.

Air

Gemini is an Air sign, Air is the element of intellect and communication, and mutable Air is the designated flight space for plausible motormouths with a deal to promote. Gemini is all talk, and can easily blarney their way out of any little local difficulties that their slacking habit gets them into.

Virgo Mutable Earth

if it moves, file it

Virgo is the second mutable sign, coming in after Leo with a broom and shovel, because they have a whole lot of lion crap to clean up. Plus they have to deal with a workforce so bedazzled by the royal touch that they need to be brought down hard to earth, obliging Libra to get off the daybed and come round to kiss them better.

The Virgo slacker style is, contrarily, very labor-intensive, but the zero results achieved from all that nitpicking and micromanagement never compute with all the hours Virgo puts in, so they might as well not have bothered.

Earth

Virgo is an Earth sign, Earth is the element of materialism, but mutable Earth is the cause of tectonic-plate shifting. Virgo likes to tamper and fiddle, and sift and separate, until things fall apart in their hands, leaving nothing but a fine coating of dust, which they have to scrub at obsessively in order to atone.

Mission statement

To incessantly sweat the small stuff until everyone wants to kill you.

Virgo slackers

Sean Connery
Ivan the Terrible
Mother Teresa
Michael Jackson

Sagittarius Mutable Fire

there'll be fireworks

Sagittarius is the third mutable sign, dashing in to break the Scorpio power beam that is immobilizing everyone's will, and then throwing such a loud, raucous celebratory party that the office burns down and Capricorn is called in to stop the fun and hurl everyone in the cooler for their own good.

The Sagittarius slacker style may be straightforward, but effectively undermines any work ethic. If there's nothing to do, they don't do it, but canter off to have fun. Once the rest of the workforce sees that the sky hasn't fallen in as a result, they trot off after the Pied Piper like good little rats.

Sagittarius slackers

Jim Morrison
Lucky Luciano
Walt Disney
Jane Austen

Fire

Sagittarius is a Fire sign, Fire is the element of excitable action, and mutable Fire is an out-of-control bush conflagration that could go anywhere, or burn itself out. Sagittarius ignites many flames, but doesn't bother to stick around tending them, so pretty soon it's all cold and dark again.

Mission statement

To boldly dash in all directions with no destination in mind.

PISCES Mutable Water

making waves

Pisces is the fourth mutable sign; if anything remains intact at the end of the zodiac trading year, Pisces will wear it down. It has to be ultra-changeable and ready to drift off in any direction, as it's got to sluice through and flood the strange irrigation system set up by Aquarius and cause such devastation that only something with an iron will and an ego the size of Aries could establish a beachhead and start all over again.

The Pisces slacker style is restless idling, either surfing waves created by others, or diving so deep they have to take a month off with nitrogen sickness.

Water

Pisces is a Water sign, Water is the element of sensationalist emotions, and mutable Water is the sea, one huge mass of wet cross-currents. Pisces slackers wear away the rocks of hard work with constant whingeing, rage unproductively in a self-induced temper, or just lie in a wet, stagnant heap.

Mission statement

To cravenly avoid commitment and responsibility until signed off to rehab on fantasy island.

Pisces slackers

Michelangelo Buonarotti

L. Ron Hubbard

Jack Kerouac

Johnny Cash

Capricorn

℃

December 22–January 20
Line Manager: Saturn

A cold, hard, tiny heart and a tight fist are the traditional basic requirements for this challenging position, but candidates without accredited qualifications in Insatiable Ambition and Obsession with Status will not be considered. Previous experience as a tyrant is desirable, and candidates who bring their own treadmill are preferred. Applicants should arrive at interview 30 minutes ahead of schedule to switch off the heating and distribute their own 156-page questionnaire, then penalize the interview panel for being late. There will be an exam on workforce intimidation and slave-driving. A relentless application of minor regulations (including amendments, subclauses, and exemptions) to all aspects of work is desirable. Positive thinkers need not apply.

Workaholics

Founder member of WA: one day at a time. Your home PCs are networked into your workstation for rapid response, and your family is down as a tax-deductible capital expenditure.

Show me the money

A respectable salary is your inalienable right, but you're more interested in annual increments, stock options, and a rock-solid pension that will pay out when you reach the top of the mountain.

Excuses, excuses

You'd have to be clinically dead before you didn't come in; it would encourage slacking. If you really can't make it, it's because you have worn out both knees groveling to the boss.

comatose   laid back   hands off   hands on   hands round   control   out of contr

the daily grind

respect my authority

It doesn't matter what the work is, as long as it revolves around a greasy pole for you to climb, because although you show the world the dull, neat exterior of a harmless drudge, inside you seethe with the kind of high-voltage ambition the Macbeths could only dream of. On the way up, you brown-nose whoever is on the rung above, while trampling on the heads of those poor saps who gave you a leg-up in the early days, or whose good ideas you have passed off as your own. When hoisted to middle management levels, you spend most of your time issuing directives demanding respect for your authority (you say you are simply ensuring respect for your rank, but that wouldn't be true, would it now?) and devising glorious Five Year Plans that only you can administer.

Your aim is power, not glory. Caution is your middle name—you don't want to be the figurehead, because you've seen what happens to figureheads (they snap off in stormy weather). Stay safe at number two—you get to make all the real decisions (the ones that make life hell for all those smart-asses who dissed you on the lower slopes); plus, in a dubious organization, when it's time to fight the law, you can simply say you were following orders.

Capricorn workstation

Oh for the days when the Deputy Assistant Administrator (grade II) had their own office. Now you have to maintain standards with the largest desk you can requisition. Your Very Important Pens are chained to your empty in-tray; your screensaver is a slideshow of past spreadsheets.

If anyone criticizes your work, you set your teeth grimly, and rush back to your workstation, from where you fire off a flurry of pompous overdetailed e-mails, copying in everybody (including the janitorial staff) pointing out that you are right and they are wrong. All this gets you nothing but mocked in the bar after work.

Bad timing

You get into the office that strategic half hour before everyone else, so that you can be seen doing conspicuous data-processing as the boss walks in. This makes the rest of the workforce feel surly and inadequate—just how you like it.

How employable are you?

Boringly so. Goats will eat anything—and you will do any job—as long as it has a large enough workforce for you to feel self-important; a complicated hierarchy of advancement that saps everyone's will to live; and a proper name badge. Any kind of financial organization welcomes you warmly: you are very creative with the small print, and implacable in the face of distressed war widows and orphans, but organized crime can be just as satisfactory (although without the name badge).

Mental health day count

Zero. Someone else might take your place on the ladder.

Dream jobs for Capricorn

So what should you do in the ideal Capricorn world of work? What would suit you best and inflict the least harm on everyone else?

Loss adjustor

Excellent: sneering at people who fitted substandard burglar alarms or forget to turn off the oven, writing damning reports so that insurance companies can pay out on the Scrooge scale (and as late as possible).

Mao Zedong

Politician

A natural choice for a self-opinionated status junkie with the stamina to do all the boring grunt work on dull subcommittees finally gets you into office, when you can draft laws to make us all behave your way.

Role model

Mao Zedong (December 26, 1893). Ruthless peasant librarian who fought his way slowly up the bamboo pole to become the ruler of the People's Republic of China, punishing everyone who deviated to the left or right of his path. You are not worthy.

office politics

professional foul

You like to think you are really good at this. Look at your fellow Capricorn role models: Stalin. Mao. Tricky Dicky. You may be pompous and mockworthy, but being Mr./Ms. Stuffy is a smart way to destabilize your enemies into underestimating you. If there is opposition to your plans, you encourage it, politely ask people to submit suggestions in writing (let a hundred flowers bloom!), then pick off the self-incriminating traitors in batches, preferably in a boardroom show trial where you turn up with damning piles of paperwork you prepared earlier. It all goes wrong when your congenital inflexibility kicks in and you refuse to move fast enough to dodge the bullets, or get too smug to notice the coup being planned by your own secret police.

Backstabbing

It's a criminal waste of training time and recruitment costs to off an employee who has crossed you; far more cost-effective (and satisfactory) to hound them to a chilly Gulag in the basement, refuse to authorize vacation leave, and work them in the data mines until they drop.

Brown-nose index

High. There's nothing wrong with obscene groveling if that's what it takes to climb a little higher. Where's the percentage in flouncing off in High Moral Outrage just because the new line manager is a born-again douche-bag? Much easier to cut off their oxygen supply when you are on top. It's not hypocrisy, it's timing.

You and the greasy pole

A ladder seems hardly big enough to service your kind of ambition. It's corporate mountaineering for you, and the more pan-global the organization, the better. You've got a good head for heights, your neat little feet can fit into the tiniest crevice of advancement, and you love living on C rations and snow-water. You'll spend as long as it takes on the windy outcrop of the second rung waiting for conditions to be right to take the summit, either by head-butting your rivals when no one's looking or by waiting for the company founder to die and leave you the entire conglomerate.

Watercooler moment

You only go there to condemn idle gossip—but only after you have written it all down in your little black notebook.

office fun

who would have thought it?

Life is a serious business and you are a graduate of the prestigious Saturn Business School, so you come on like the company Hall Monitor, patrolling the cubicles to make sure nobody comes out unless they have a boardroom pass. Plus any group fun after hours might involve spending money, and you know how nervous that makes you; you've been banned from the office bar because you bring your own turnip wine. However ... sometimes there is a dawn raid by old Saturn (the one who invented Saturnalia) and you astound coworkers by ringleading something really naughty, like duct-taping the boss to his chair during his power nap. You get away with it because management simply don't believe that dull, tiny-hearted you would do such a thing.

Office romance

I did mention that you will do anything to get ahead—and this is one of them. Catch you falling for anyone, just because of the way the light from the OHP drifts across their cheekbones. A total status slut, you're hot for anybody who can upgrade your career (or knows someone who can). These are not always the obvious suspects. It's worth putting in the flirt hours with the dermatologically challenged dork in Acquisitions, because you know their mom is best friends with the boss's sister

ISBN 0-670-04219-6

9 780670 042197

Dress-down disasters

How will anyone know how important you are if you're not wearing a dark suit that screams authority? But it is company policy (until you clamber into the boss's seat), so you loosen your tie or undo the top two buttons of your Agnès b.

Office party

You raincheck office parties because you are terrified of the Inner Goat that busts out after a few snorts of cheap red, dances like a satyr on steroids, spikes the Virgin Manhattans, and kicks down the door to the executive washroom, with the CEO in one hand and a mirror and a razor blade in the other. And you avoid team-bonding weekends because cross-rank fraternization leads to low morale.

Your cheapest trick

Probably the one where you sack any old retainers who've been with the company since it started, especially around Christmas time. Otherwise none—you don't do anti-gravitas. But few colleagues can resist supergluing a target to your back and following you around all day taking snaps of you on their cellphones.

teamwork

on your terms

On Corporate World being in a team is essential—but it has to be a successful team, otherwise you will not Get On. So you go into methodology overdrive, generating a blizzard of schedules, timetables, agendas, and Guidelines to Best Practice, and call people sitting next to you to tell them you have sent an e-mail reminding them about the memo you circulated last week. When there is a failure of discipline, you take it upon yourself to point out that the guilty party has let down themselves, the team, and the company (clichés have never bothered you) and, if they still snicker at you, file a formal complaint and smirk insufferably when their desk is cleared. So what if no one speaks to you for a month afterward? You have work to do.

Leader, follower, passenger, grunt

It's your long-term plan to be leader, but it often takes you so long to get there that it's too late. You are happy to slipstream as a follower, making considerable savings on fuel costs, but only as far as the upper slopes. No one wants you as a passenger; you have no talent for idling gracefully, and sulk because they won't use your sat nav. You make a good grunt (it's Base Camp to you, not a dead end), but are usually sacked because middle management don't want to be outclassed by a smartypants barrack-room lawyer.

Know your enemies

Aries—their horns are bigger than yours, so head-butt them into the gulch from behind.

Taurus—whip them all you like, they're never going to pull the plow any faster.

Gemini—they are Road Runner, you are Wile E. Coyote; you'll never catch up.

Cancer—your opposite sign: luckily they go sideways, not up, so no immediate threat.

Leo—play nice, they may be connected and able to boost you to a higher ledge.

Virgo—memo wars: yours are important need-to-knows, theirs are tiny-minded rants.

Libra—you'll always do all the work, they'll always steal all the credit; get over it.

Scorpio—you won't win this one; take the money and start another company.

Sagittarius—don't waste precious work hours trying to force them to respect you.

Capricorn—as rabidly ambitious as you; double death-plunge from the top floor?

Aquarius—post the daily disciplinary e-mails you send them on their MySpace page.

Pisces—life's too short to listen to all the dumb excuses, so just do their work yourself.

Are you talking to me?

In triplicate. Very long, complicated orders in disturbingly neat handwriting, bristling with subclauses, footnotes, exemptions, and addenda, are posted twice daily. No one has the will to read them, so there is never any feedback.

Worst-case scenario

From the company's POV, a team of Capricorns sounds good, but is so slow, thorough, and inflexible on the ground that it drags the entire operation kicking and screaming into the 19th century. Send in Aquarius alpha-geeks with a time machine.

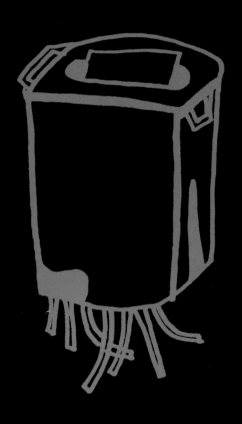

Aquarius

≋

January 21–February 18
Line Manager: Uranus

If you are an offbeat loner with Arctic levels of dispassionate disdain for the work ethic, the zodiac needs you, but only if you can demonstrate that you do not need the zodiac. A Masters in Chilly Detachment will be an advantage, and a track record of hands-off experience is essential. Eccentric contrariness is a core skill. If they can be assed, candidates should shamble to interview wearing a T-shirt with the official Aquarius logo, DILLIGAF (Do I look like I Give a F@?%?), on prominent display, and remain outside the interview room throughout to demonstrate the required levels of Insolent Independence. People persons need not apply. This post is part of a positive-selection program for the routine-phobic with an incurable allergy to conventional behavior.

Workaholics

Depends. You usually go for an underpowered job that uses so few brain bytes you've forgotten all about it the minute you sign off. If it's a dream job, it's not work and you'll never go home

Show me the money

While you are far too cool to be seen getting heated about money, you need to service your gadget habit; luckily you've designed a bit of software that lets you print off as many bills as you need

Excuses, excuses

When you don't show for work it's because you're busy playing Halo or have broken a hip tripping over the cat's cradle of cables that serve your home surveillance system

the daily grind

you cannot be serious

Frankly, you'd rather be spending your time on your pioneering research/time machine/ Great American Novel/art installation, but a waterboy's gotta drink, and if you don't have state funding or private patronage, any old McJob will do. This has nothing to do with your abilities—infuriatingly, you can work out the OS of any job in about 10 seconds. It didn't take you long to work out that every admin job, however high-powered

or uptitled, is just a variation on the basic Filing Template. If offered the kind of high-profile post that comes with a mega salary and a level of prestige presidents would kill for, you will, of course, turn it down with a contemptuous snort as you hate to be obvious and despise status junkies.

Imaginative bosses (one of life's natural minorities) appreciate you because you don't have to be told to think outside the box—you hurled the box into the recycling dumpster the minute that you arrived. Unimaginative bosses hate you because they suspect, rightly, that you could do their job in your sleep if you felt like it, and they lie awake at night wondering why you don't feel like it. So you are regularly preemptively sacked (usually in your absence, because you can't be assed to remember your shift dates), but you don't care.

Aquarius workstation

You like to emphasize your otherness by lining the walls of your remote cubicle with BacoFoil® or installing a pop-up one-person tent. Peripherals sprout from both computers, and you perch happily on your upturned beer crate, running the spyware that lets you observe the rest of us.

If any one criticizes your work, you stare straight through them, act like they're not even there, and walk away. If you think they're worth rational opposition, you come on like Cyrano de Bergerac and cut them down to size with a withering list of their own shortcomings, all noted down as background for your forthcoming experimental short on workplace psychosis.

Bad timing

You refuse to follow anyone else's agenda, so never turn up on time or even on day. You've put in hours establishing your absent-minded genius/troubadour/poet persona so no one will bother you with all that tedious clock-watching business.

How employable are you?

Barely. There's not a lot of call for sarcastic, insolent routine-phobes who spit on the corporate ethic, loathe being overseen, customize the uniform (and not in a good way) and get surly filling out those self-appraisal forms when it's review time.

Your tetchy sneer means that anything involving interfacing with the customer base is out. Best sign up as a techie, because only other techies know what you are talking about, and the boss can't tell whether you are working or not and daren't ask.

Mental health day count

High. You're not going to stop doing anything interesting just because it's a workday.

Dream jobs for Aquarius

So what should you do in the ideal Aquarian world of work? What would suit you best and inflict the least harm on everyone else?

Croupier

They may look like toys, but the roulette wheel, dice, and pack of cards are all portals to a secret cosmos of probability, numbers, systems, and chance—and only you have the keys. For this, even you will wear a tux.

Mad scientist

Someone gives you funding to order in stacks of shiny apparatus, play around with ideas, and grow a beard (optional). All they want in return is a smallish, itsy-bitsy little doomsday weapon; what's not to like?

Role model

Lord George Byron (January 22, 1788) Career outcast and convention-busting poet, inventor of the cool, floppy-shirted, floppy-haired, mad, bad schtick; woke up famous one day without even trying, and died (perversely) of rheumatic fever fighting the Greek War of Independence. How cool!

Lord George Byron

office politics

the outsider

As a wacky obstreperous loner, it's not your style to do office politics; for a start, you'd have to give a damn, and you don't. Standing on the sidelines looking sardonic is as engagé as you like to get, and you could take up a rewarding second career as a double (or even triple) agent, if you could be bothered. No one will ever know whose side you're on, although it's a fair bet you'll support the unpopular underdog until they become popular top dog, when you'll lose interest. The strands of all boardroom plots are as obvious to you as a laser matrix, so you rarely get caught in the crossfire. Of course you could be king of the heap, but that might mean responsibility and having to suffer fools, so you don't push it.

Backstabbing

Blood on the carpet is far too gutty for you. Instead, throw some rope, teach them a hangman's knot, and watch them swing from a noose of their own making. Then take notes on how long it takes for their career to die, and pick up tips on how to improve your technique for next time.

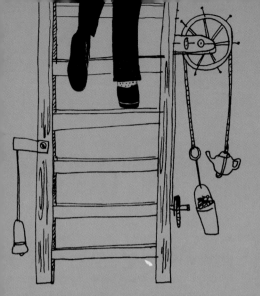

You and the greasy pole

You haven't spent your life slapping concealer on the royal birthmark and hiding the magical sword of power in the back of the closet, or covering your Vulcan ears under a beanie, just to give yourself away in a show of ambition. So you sidestep the traditional career ladder and construct one of your own in an unfashionable corner of the workplace, using skills and training picked up over the years, bolting them together in ways that would not occur to anyone else. (Realtor sans frontières?) If you get near the top, you deconstruct the entire ladder and reconfigure the elements into a whole new career.

Brown-nose index

Zero. There is no logic to undeserved flattery, you sneer loftily, as coworkers go into Fawnication Overdrive. Brighter managers deduce that you are wired up to some sort of power source (cold fusion?) they will never understand, so promote you anyway to hedge their bets. You refuse, and stalk back to the mailroom.

Watercooler moment

If you're so cool, how come you hang around this gossip hotbed? To study lower life forms in their natural habitat—that's why.

offiçε fun

what's the alternative?

You're one of three signs headhunted from your original planets by aggressive new cosmic upstarts—in your case, Uranus. You've heard all the jokes, thanks, and often have to call on the advanced grump-and-surl skills you picked up at Saturn, Inc. (your old firm) to deal with coworkers who just won't let it go. The upside is that Uranus is the planet of lateral thinking, bizarre behavior, and tediously surreal combinations, so you are the office alternative comedian, famous for your deadpan one-liners and sustained surreal riffs (do paperclips feel pain?). Your own idea of fun is to improve your screentan by logging on to the fantasy forum you built when no one was looking; you are Dungeon Master in the specially adapted RPG, *Dungeons and Deadlines*.

Office romance

You don't do office romance, not because of any 'burby moralistic values, but because you don't do any kind of romance. All that physical neediness—no, thanks. So you are often a bit besieged, especially by Aries and Gemini, who like a challenge. You don't notice, as you are signing in to one of your 20 online dating sites (a different name, gender, and avatar for each). What you want is an online partner, in tight underwear and a couple of time zones away, so you don't have to meet.

Dress-down disasters

Everyone wonders how you will be able to dress down your everyday time-traveling-surfer-pirate thing, but you can't resist subverting a stereotype, so if you ever do make it in on Friday, you are pin-sharp in Prada and pristine John Lobbs/Ferragamos.

Office party

After sneering at the office do, you turn up, stand aloof in a corner like Oscar Wilde at a frat party, get altered states-ish on your own cocktails (absinthe and chocolate malt), and crack wise with one of the big-spending clients, just to see the boss sweat. You sneer at group bonding weekends, but turn up, because how can you show how different you are from the group unless you are in a group?

Your cheapest trick

Big Brother is a favorite. You stride with a clipboard and a ladder into departments where they don't know you, install fake webcams in every cubicle, then stand back and take notes as productivity surges for at least two weeks. Of course, only you are in on the joke, but since when did that matter?

teamwork

rebel, rebel

Every team (group, ensemble, rockband) has to field the obligatory touchy loner, the ornery rebel without a subclause, the odd one who insists on going up life's down escalators. The A-Team had Murdock, the *American Pie* high schoolers had Finch, *The Taming of the Shrew* had Petruchio—your office has got you. Smart team leaders try to harness your offbeat methods when doing it by the book just doesn't deliver, but you can't stand being managed, so you scupper the plan by turning into Mr./Ms. Conventionality overnight. Of course, you're aware of the team mission, but you'll get there in your own way; anyone who thinks Taurus is stubborn hasn't seen you in Full Recalcitrance Mode. You don't give anyone up; that would be pandering to the Man.

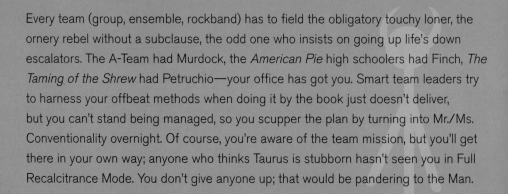

Leader, follower, passenger, grunt

Never a leader (even though you would be brilliant, since you know everything): you can't handle all those trustful little faces looking up at you for direction. Follower? I don't think so; you'll only ever move to your own beat, and that's always hip-hop when everyone else is line-dancing. You can be a really irritating passenger—the one who knows the way, but won't tell the driver. Brightsiders have you down as the zodiac's democrat, and you like singing along with the common people, but preferably not in the same room. Grunts love you, but you wish they wouldn't slobber.

Know your enemies

Aries—deflect all that crude bullying by talking back in Estonian/Xhosa/Navajo.

Taurus—twin obstinacy orbits: they won't step out of their rut, you won't step in.

Gemini—you don't have any allies they can turn against you, which makes them mad.

Cancer—make their shell shake by telling them the deadline's been brought forward.

Leo—your opposite sign; the Darth Vader to your leader of the Rebel Alliance.

Virgo—they won't bother you; the heaps of fast-food wrappers make them nauseous.

Libra—wear mirrored shades to distract them from work with their own reflections.

Scorpio—hack into their laptop and mess with their agendas—it freaks them out.

Sagittarius—get some quiet time by daring them to eat everything in the shredder.

Capricorn—apply for all the same internal promotions they do, just to get their goat.

Aquarius—there's only room for one wacky loner in any workplace; terminate the clone.

Pisces—stop them stealing your ideas by writing them up in invisible ink.

Are you talking to me?

You communicate by mumbling or MSN, and in code: Java, html, Morse, geekspeak, or your own made-up office esperanto, otherwise ordinary people might understand. No one can decode your instructions well enough to offer feedback.

Worst-case scenario

From the company's POV, a team of Aquarians could revolutionize the place, the way Lenin revolutionized Russia. Not to worry: the team will factionalize and destroy itself with infighting before any Capricorn Riot Squads are sent in.

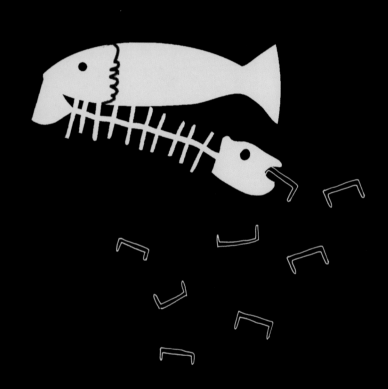

PISCES

⟩(⟨

February 19–March 20
Line Manager: Neptune

As the world owes Pisces a living, Zodiac Inc. is obliged to offer an undemanding, fish-centric post especially created to suit the Piscean skill set (whining, neediness, tetchiness, spite, and dependency). Applicants must have graduated in Slippery Manipulation Studies, or at least claim that they have, and been selected to try out for Reality Dodging at international level. The ability to blame everyone else for everything is essential. Lies, evasion, denials, contradictory mood swings, and wet-eyed sentimentality are core skills. Candidates should only apply because someone else told them to, drift in late for interview and at the wrong place, hand in a fantasy résumé, then institute a lawsuit for negligent discrimination when they don't get the job.

Workaholics

Career Cilohakrow. (See what I did there?) There's never enough time to finish all the things you have to do at home actually at home, so of course you bring them to the office with you.

Show me the money

Other people have made you spend all your advances for the year, plus bonuses, so now you have to get creative with expenses—it's all Accounting's fault for letting you handle your own money.

Excuses, excuses

The MySpace page with your killer excuses listing gets a trillion hits a day—you'll get a publishing deal any day now. The one about dropping a jeroboam of champagne on your toes is true, though.

comatose   laid back   hands off   hands on   hands round   control   out of contr

the daily grind

the curse of the drinking classes

No one understands your pain. You are an artiste. It may say "Customer service operative" in your job description, but you are in fact a misunderstood genius. Brightsiders say you are creative, which is just salon talk for unemployable, so you think this gives you license to stare blankly at the wall for hours at a time, or even close your eyes to await the muse. The snoring is always a giveaway, plus the slumping slack-jawed and drooling onto your desk. You are ambitious, though, and want to get on, as long as it does not involve actually doing anything. You talk a great job, blagging your way through strategy meetings (like you do strategy!) with convincingly detailed reference to statistics, case studies, and field research (all validated by your alma mater, the Institute of Making It Up As You Go Along) and bits of baffling business-speak like "front-end methodology loading" (which you made up). But when it comes to follow-through and implementation, you slide away with the tide. When you are not praised extravagantly by everybody for the work you imagine you've done (it's like a phantom limb to you—all the pain but nothing to show for it), you feel very hard done by, and sulk, bitch, and go off to the bar for the rest of the day.

Pisces workstation

Every cubicle is exactly the same, but yours is never quite right—the light's wrong, it's too hot, it's too cold, you can't work with colored walls, you can hear the person next door breathing. Unstructured heaps of paperwork and fluffy toys shelter your JD bottles (purely medicinal).

If anyone criticizes your work, or asks why you haven't actually done anything except play online poker since the day you started the job, you flap your fins, bluster, crank up the whinge engine, start sobbing about how you are overworked and anyway you haven't been well lately, and blame everybody else for not recognizing your sensitive nature.

Bad timing

You're not late, as such, and are regularly in by late afternoon. Anyway, it's not your fault. You got lost. Someone told you it was Sunday. There was a rogue rhinoceros on the subway and it ate the presentation. You promise to go home on time.

How employable are you?

Is there anything you can actually do? Well, not a lot. You should never work with chainsaws or heavy machinery, or in anything like neurosurgery or air traffic control, where concentration and a steady hand are essential. Nor should you be trusted in any of the caring professions—obviously a ruse to get near to the pharmaceuticals. No one in their right mind would make you an executive anything, unless they had a secret plan to run the company into the ground for tax reasons.

Mental health day count

Stratospheric. Every day is an intolerable strain to hypersensitive you. They're lucky you come in at all.

Dream jobs for Pisces

So what should you do in the ideal Piscean world of work? What would suit you best and inflict the least harm on everyone else?

Shaman

A legitimate reason to get off your face on exotic substances and lie around in a trance dreaming, while the rest of the village feed your family and clean your house. You're doing it for others—it's not your fault.

Albert Einstein

Tabloid TV talkshow host

A prepaid trip on the Emotional Tourist bus, with a stopover at Vicarious Wallowing; you love to help, and in return you get unconditional appreciation and killer ratings. Feel the gratitude in the room!

Role model

Albert Einstein (March 14, 1879). He spent his early working life in an obscure Patent Office, dreaming up a fantastic theory to explain how time is not the solid commodity people think it is, and that truth is relative—just as you have always maintained.

office politics

murky waters

Look, it's not that you are a lying, cheating, conniving, devious, fickle, manipulative, disloyal flake: it just looks that way because you are the office neo-con, not at home to reality-based scenarios or inconvenient facts, and living your own version of the fish bowl. This means that you flicker about being all things to all people, changing direction on a dime, because it doesn't matter to you which way the tide's going. Whatever political knot your department gets itself into, you will always wriggle free (it's the great plus of being so bendy) and escape to calm waters, either with a golden handshake or a corner office. And so what if you go down with the ship: it makes you look good and noble, and you can swim out of any wreckage.

Backstabbing

There is no need to get your hands dirty or work too hard at this; activate the tyranny of the weak. Spend a few lunchtimes spreading insinuations, accuse the enemy of unspecified harassment, cry in board meetings, and wait until they feel obliged to commit office seppuku. Banzai!

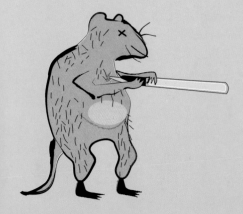

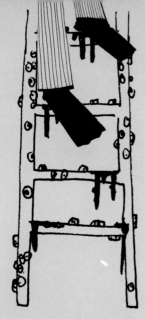

You and the greasy pole

It's not your fault that you don't get on as well as your many talents indicate that you ought to, but rather flap around the career ladder, slide off unexpectedly, and can't seem to get a grip. How can you be expected to climb something so obviously not designed for a person with fins and no discernible backbone? It's blatant rung-ist, workplace discrimination against fishkind in general (and you in particular). You demand the provision of bucket access, so that you can be carried up to the top by differently abled coworkers.

Brown-nose index

Best Supporting, after Libra. Your preferred method is the Adorable Puppy/Fluffy Kitty maneuver, where you stare sincerely at the mark with round-eyed devotion, snuffle/purr, and wind yourself around their legs (not always metaphorically) until they have to reward you with a cookie or promotion, and feel bad when they have to discipline you.

Watercooler moment

Pull up a bar stool and waste some quality time (theirs) telling everyone how you could have been a contender.

office fun

i'm at the office, get me outta here

One of your prioritized objectives is fun—or at least, not work. Are you not the most successful brand strategist at Escapism Solutions, Inc.? Although you did your basic training with Jupiter, the work ethic was a bit too gung-ho and you were soon offloaded to Neptune, niche purveyor of indolence and hangovers, a much better fit. You are amazingly organized about fun, and work harder at scamming freebies and creating reasons to be out of the office than you do at actual work. You are the office bar-spotter, and put in the hours finding somewhere that will give you a discount for netting the custom. If you absolutely can't get away (apparently it's a really important meeting), you download every series of *Lost* on to your laptop and drift away.

Office romance

Get it while you can, and wherever you are. You need saturation adoration, so even if you have a partner (or several) in civilian life, it won't stop you angling for more at the office. You don't want to work too hard, so target the plain and inept—the ones you think will be most grateful—and lure them out for lost afternoons at their expense. But you soon lose interest, blame them for being boring, and drift along to the next one. You get away with it because they are too ashamed to make a fuss.

Dress-down disasters

It's hard enough for you to get dressed on your own every day, and you whine about the extra pressure—until you realize you can spend Thursday night out, and come in next day without having to worry about whose clothes you are wearing.

Office party

Any office do means a chance to play your favorite sport—bobbing for olives—for free, so you are there at the off. After a couple of hours in maximum charm mode, your mood does a 180, and you start duking it out with Aries. It's a relief for everyone when you pass out under the table. You sign up for all the bonding courses; any excuse to get away from responsibilities at home.

Your cheapest trick

Annoying windups are your thing. There's nothing funnier than telling social mountaineer Capricorn that the boss is secretly in love with him, and that he should grow a goatee and wear orange Argyll socks to the next production meeting to show that he loves her right back. (All right, so you ripped it off from *Twelfth Night*; so sue you.)

teamwork

sweet shoal music

Slippery and unreliable, you are not first pick for a team. Incessant mood swings make you impossible to work with; you'll never damage your silver sheen by doing anything committed, like pulling your weight; and when the going gets tough, you just drift away. You can only do anything if there is instant gratification every few minutes, as there is for pilot fish scavenging snacks from between a shark's teeth. You'll turn anyone in, with an Emmy award-winning show of reluctance, but only by anonymous e-mail or when you are alone with the boss, because it upsets you to embarrass the guilty party in front of the rest of the team (and you can't risk them noisily pointing out that it was really you who diverted the entire project budget into your own pocket).

Leader, follower, passenger, grunt

Disastrous as a leader: the minute you make up your mind, you change it, then flounce into a towering strop because no one is doing what you ordered. Follower? Now you're talking—you'll follow anybody, because whatever you do (however dreadful), it will be their fault. You make an even better passenger, surfing along on the efforts of others. Even that stresses you out, so you're better going with the flow of grunts and getting away with doing nothing except make up the numbers.

Know your enemies

Aries—it's not fair: they shouted at you, so now you're too fragile to lift a pencil.

Taurus—it's their fault you're late; they should have lent you their alarm clock.

Gemini—it's not fair: they stole that great campaign concept you stole from Aquarius.

Cancer—it's their fault you're off sick; they asked you to clean up your desk.

Leo—it's not fair: they get all the attention in meetings just because they're the boss.

Virgo—your opposite sign, so everything you're not; it's all their fault.

Libra—it's not fair: they do even less than you do and never get shouted at.

Scorpio—it's their fault you've crashed the system; they looked at you in a funny way.

Sagittarius—it's not fair: they made you play online poker with the clients' money.

Capricorn—it's their fault you're a nervous wreck; they made you work from 9 till 5:30.

Aquarius—it's not fair: you slept through their IT seminar, so now you can't log on.

Pisces—it's their fault you're still in the bar; they're in charge of counting the Martinis.

Are you talking to me?

Coworkers record any interchange with you because, whatever you say, you say the complete opposite almost immediately. You strenuously deny what's on record. Whatever you say that isn't fantasy is lies, so feedback is a waste of time.

Worst-case scenario

From the company's POV, a team of Pisceans means sending Virgo out with a clean-up team to scour the area bars, until you are found in a pool of codependent degradation. It will take a coalition of Earth signs to get you back to work.

Instant Career Selector

If you are really unhappy in your work, maybe it's not just your curmudgeonly attitude; perhaps you should be in a job more suited to your Darkside. You've already seen what your dream jobs could be: this helpful Instant Career Selector lists further career options—both legal(ish) and criminal—by sign, for quick and easy reference. Consult it when you can't stand another day in the battery farm, or when interfering busybodies who are not your mom ask you pointed questions like: When exactly are you going to get an actual job—and as what?

Aries

Aries career choices should be hot on mindlessly physical action and, if possible, should involve fire, metal, and/or shouting.

Legal(ish)

★ Corporate raider

★ Boot-camp sergeant

★ Oil-fire supremo

★ Dictator

★ Prize fighter

★ Roadie

Criminal

★ Henchman

★ Arsonist

★ Ram raider

★ Burglar

★ Safe blower

★ Gangster

Do not go anywhere near

the nursing professions, counseling, facilitating, precision engineering, mediation services, or conflict resolution.

Taurus

Taurus career choices should focus strongly on stuff—money, food, territory—how to get lots of it and how to hang on to it.

Legal(ish)

★ Tyrant

★ Bounty hunter

★ Tax collector

★ Meat wholesaler

★ Bailiff

★ Door-to-door salesperson

Criminal

★ Bank robber

★ Art rustler

★ Hit man

★ Torturer

★ Treasure hunter

★ Black marketeer

Do not go anywhere near

anything that requires flexibility, irregular shift work, freelancing, or international diplomacy.

Gemini

Gemini career choices should take full advantage of this sign's instant reflexes and ability to talk their way out of anything.

Legal(ish)

★ Telesales operative

★ Futures broker

★ Market trader

★ Street magician

★ Tax lawyer

★ PR guru

Criminal

★ Gun runner

★ Blackmailer

★ Jewel thief

★ Drug smuggler

★ Con artist

★ Gangster's moll

Do not go anywhere near

filing, routine, long periods of sitting still, jobs where people's lives depend on you.

Cancer

Cancer career choices are all about maintaining a low profile, while at the same time showing who's boss.

Legal(ish)

★ Supernanny

★ Chef

★ Lighthouse keeper

★ Ghost writer

★ Puppeteer

★ Sleuth

Criminal

★ Poisoner

★ Smuggler

★ Kidnapper

★ Poison-pen writer

★ Capo di capi

★ Loan shark

Do not go anywhere near

anything that needs a cunning plan carried out on time and on budget, the confrontational professions, or being seen in public.

Leo

Leo career choices are about showing off and being seen and worshipped by as many people as possible.

Legal(ish)

★ Monarch

★ Media mogul

★ Sugar daddy

★ Goldmine owner

★ Circus ringmaster

★ WWE wrestler

Criminal

★ Bullion thief

★ Grand scammer

★ Snake-oil salesman

★ Hustler

★ Gang leader

★ Identity thief

Do not go anywhere near

the secret service, covert ops, or closed religious orders.

Virgo

Virgo career choices should involve routine, data processing, and an obsession with patterns and detail.

Legal(ish)

★ Homeopath

★ CSI officer

★ Critic

★ Nanotechnologist

★ Sanitary engineer

★ Life coach

Criminal

★ Forger

★ Serial killer

★ Money launderer

★ Clean-up person

★ Tax evader

★ Drug distributor

Do not go anywhere near

anything sensitive, subtle, nuanced, or that hasn't been thoroughly scoured.

Libra

Libra career choices emphasize work that does not look like you're doing too much and has very high production values.

Legal(ish)

★ Odds fixer

★ Entertainment lawyer

★ Gigolo

★ Trophy wife

★ Used-car dealer

★ Sleep researcher

Criminal

★ Fluffer

★ Credit-card skimmer

★ Fence

★ Industrial spy

★ Diamond smuggler

★ Grifter

Do not go anywhere near

construction work, coal mining, ship building or heavy engineering, or cheap and nasty retail outlets.

Scorpio

Scorpio career choices focus on control, secrecy, wealth—and more control.

Legal(ish)

★ Secret agent

★ Political guru

★ Interrogator

★ Funeral director

★ Samurai

★ Vampire slayer

Criminal

★ Porn star

★ Sex worker

★ Drug baron

★ Internet pirate

★ Dominatrix

★ Mastermind

Do not go anywhere near

global corporations that you do not own, woo-woo businesses, or the caring professions.

Sagittarius

Sagittarian career options must involve constant movement, high adrenaline levels, physical contact, and random risk factors.

Legal(ish)

★ Gambler

★ Card shark

★ Rock star

★ Gopher

★ Bike messenger

★ Crocodile wrangler

Criminal

★ Pimp

★ Mugger

★ Rustler

★ Outlaw

★ Getaway driver

★ Carjacker

Do not go anywhere near

the caring professions, libraries, or data-processing operations.

Capricorn

Capricorn career options should focus on sensible, lucrative, permanent jobs with a fat pension and stock options.

Legal(ish)

★ IRS inspector

★ Horror-story writer

★ Offshore banker

★ Goatherd

★ Mountaineer

★ Prison guard

Criminal

★ Insider dealer

★ Despot

★ Extortionist

★ Embezzler

★ Satanist

★ Grave robber

Do not go anywhere near

professions with no discernible career path, anywhere with open-plan offices and a workers' ball bath in the atrium, or big-time charities.

Aquarius

Aquarius career options should only be apparent to Aquarians; everyone else expects you to be a mad scientist, so don't be.

Legal(ish)

★ Astronaut

★ Surveillance installer

★ Professional revolutionary

★ Poet

★ Microserf

★ SF convention convener

Criminal

★ Stalker

★ Hacker

★ Sniper

★ Spy

★ Data miner

★ Cyberthief

Do not go anywhere near

anything in the real world—real estate, pension selling, heavy industry, or anything that means working 9 to 5.

Pisces

Pisces career options should take full advantage of the sign's core strengths: sensationalism, fantasy, and illusion.

Legal(ish)

★ Escape artist

★ Cult founder

★ Timeshare salesperson

★ Country and western singer

★ Mixologist

★ Aura cleanser

Criminal

★ Pirate

★ Charity scammer

★ Informer

★ Insurance fraudster

★ Crack pharmacist

★ Beggar

Do not go anywhere near

the hospitality trade, the pharmaceutical industry, chemistry, other people's money, or chainsaws.

Further Information

Books

Blaze, Chrissie, *Mercury Retrograde*, Time Warner International, 2002

Burns, Debbie, *Star Signs at Work: Using Astrology for Success and Harmony in the Workplace*, Red Wheel/Weiser, 2003

Cunningham, Donna, *How to Read Your Astrological Chart: Aspects of the Cosmic Puzzle*, Red Wheel/Weiser, 1999

Dixon-Cooper, Hazel, *Born on a Rotten Day: Illuminating and Coping with the Dark Side of the Zodiac*, Fireside, 2003.

Francis, Therese, *The Mercury Retrograde Book*, Crossquarter Breeze, 2000

Gerwick-Brodeur, Madeline, and Lenard, Lisa, *The Complete Idiot's Guide to Astrology*, Alpha Books, 2003

Lang, Adele, and Masterson, Andrew, *Bosstrology: The Twelve Bastard Bosses of the Zodiac*, Kyle Cathie, 2004

Leo, Alan, *Mars, the War Lord*, Kessinger Publishing Co., 2004

Leo, Alan, *Saturn*, Kessinger Publishing Co., 2004

Miller, Anistatia R., and Brown, Jared M., *The Complete Astrological Handbook for the 21st Century*, Schocken Books, 1999

Orion, Rae, *Astrology for Dummies*, For Dummies, 1999

Schostak, Sherene, and Iris Weiss, Stefanie, *Surviving Saturn's Return: Overcoming the Most Tumultuous Time of Your Life*, McGraw-Hill Publishing Co., 2003

Woolfolk, Joanna Martine, *The Only Astrology Book You'll Ever Need*, Madison Books, 2001

Websites

General Sites

American Federation of Astrologers
http://www.astrologers.com
The oldest astrology association in the United States, established in 1938.

Astrodienst
http://www.astro.com
A well-organized, user-friendly site set up by Swiss Alois Treindl; combines top astrologists with state-of-the-art software to bring free horoscopes, links, shopping etc.; a bit optimistic for us Darksiders, but extremely useful.

Astrolabe
http://www.alabe.com
Free computer-generated birthcharts—good for pinpointing the positions of the planets at the time of your birth. The free astrolabe interpretations are generalized, and should only be used as a starter guide.

Astrology.com
http://www.astrology.com
This site covers everything and is a good staring point if you are an astro virgin. Not everything is free, but you can sign up for various newsletters and daily updates, including the daily astroslam, which has a darkside sheen.

California Astrology Association
http://www.calastrology.com
A site that provides professional astrology readings, metaphysical products, and other services.

Café Astrology
http://www.cafeastrology.com/index.html
Tasteful, informative, easy-to-navigate site, but may be a bit too upbeat for hardcore Darksiders.

Fellow Darksiders
http://members.aol.com/httpslash/index.htm
Most astrology sites have a darkside option, but an early adopter was Black Jack Shellac. Go to this website to read about the self-styled Master of the Zodiac's dark views.

Planet-specific sites

Saturn
http://www.saturnreturn.net
An excellent site by the famous Saturn Sisters; everything you could want to know about planet work, including how to deal with Saturn's return. Designed primarily for women, although of course Saturn itself is not gender specific.

Mercury
http://www.astroprofile.com/2007mercuryrx.htm
A practical site with exact information about when Mercury goes retrograde. Get ahead of the game by scheduling in the next backwards period and taking precautions; it won't stop the chaos, but you'll look good.

Index

Air 6
  Aquarius 101
  Gemini 140
  Libra 58
alabe.com 12
Aquarius 101,
  156–67
  career selector 187
  opposite number
    14–15
Ares 12
Aries 18–29, 56
  career selector 182
  Mars 12
  opposite number
    14–15
at work
  Aquarius 159–60
  Aries 29–2
  Cancer 63–4
  Capricorn 147–8
  Gemini 45–6
  Leo 75–6
  Libra 105–6
  Pisces 171–2
  Sagittarius 129–30
  Scorpio 117–18
  Taurus 33–4
  Virgo 87–8

backstabbing
  Aquarius 162
  Aries 24
  Cancer 66
  Capricorn 150
  Gemini 48
  Leo 78
  Libra 108
  Pisces 174

  Sagittarius 132
  Scorpio 120
  Taurus 36
  Virgo 90
Billy the Kid 131
brown-nose index
  Aquarius 163
  Aries 25
  Cancer 67
  Capricorn 151
  Gemini 49
  Leo 79
  Libra 109
  Pisces 175
  Sagittarius 133
  Scorpio 121
  Taurus 37
  Virgo 91
Byron, Lord George
  161

Cancer 57, 60–71
  career selector 183
  opposite number
    14–15
Capricorn 59,
  144–55
  career selector 186
  opposite number
    14–15
Saturn 10
cardinal quality 6, 14,
  54–9
career ladder
  Aquarius 163
  Aries 25
  Cancer 67
  Capricorn 151
  Gemini 49

Leo 79
Libra 109
Pisces 175
Sagittarius 133
Scorpio 121
Taurus 37
Virgo 91
career selector
  180–7
Che Guevara 47
clothes
  Aquarius 165
  Aries 27
  Cancer 69
  Capricorn 153
  Gemini 51
  Leo 81
  Libra 111
  Pisces 177
  Sagittarius 135
  Scorpio 123
  Taurus 39
  Virgo 93
communication
  Aquarius 167
  Aries 29
  Cancer 71
  Capricorn 155
  Gemini 53
  Leo 83
  Libra 113
  Pisces 179
  Sagittarius 137
  Scorpio 125
  Taurus 41
  Virgo 95
Cronos 11

dream jobs
  Aquarius 161
  Aries 23
  Cancer 65
  Capricorn 149
  Gemini 47
  Leo 77
  Libra 107
  Pisces 173
  Sagittarius 131
  Scorpio 119
  Taurus 35
  Virgo 89

Earth 6
  Capricorn 59
  Taurus 98
  Virgo 141
Einstein, Albert 173
Elizabeth I 89
employability
  Aquarius 160
  Aries 22
  Cancer 64
  Capricorn 148
  Gemini 46
  Leo 76
  Libra 106
  Pisces 172
  Sagittarius 130
  Scorpio 118
  Taurus 34
  Virgo 88
enemies
  Aquarius 167
  Aries 29
  Cancer 71
  Capricorn 155
  Gemini 53

Leo 83
Libra 113
Pisces 179
Sagittarius 137
Scorpio 125
Taurus 41
Virgo 95

Fire 6
  Aries 56
  Leo 99
  Sagittarius 142
fixed quality 6, 14,
  96–101
followers
  Aquarius 166
  Aries 28
  Cancer 70
  Capricorn 154
  Gemini 52
  Leo 82
  Libra 112
  Pisces 178
  Sagittarius 136
  Scorpio 124
  Taurus 40
  Virgo 94
fun
  Aquarius 164–5
  Aries 26–7
  Cancer 68–9
  Capricorn 152–3
  Gemini 50–1
  Leo 80–1
  Libra 110–11
  Pisces 176–7
  Sagittarius 134–5
  Scorpio 122–3
  Taurus 38–9

Virgo 92–3

Gemini 42–53, 140
  career selector 183
  Mercury 13
  opposite number
    14–15
grunts
  Aquarius 166
  Aries 28
  Cancer 70
  Capricorn 154
  Gemini 52
  Leo 82
  Libra 112
  Pisces 178
  Sagittarius 136
  Scorpio 124
  Taurus 40
  Virgo 94

Henry VIII 65
hot desking 21

Khan, Genghis 35

leadership
  Aquarius 166
  Aries 28, 56
  Cancer 57, 70
  Capricorn 59, 154
  Gemini 52
  Leo 82
  Libra 58, 112
  natural born bosses
    54–9
  Pisces 178
  Sagittarius 136
  Scorpio 124

Taurus 40
Virgo 94
Leo 72–83, 99
  career selector 184
  opposite number
    14–15
  Saturn 10
Leonardo da Vinci 23
Libra 58, 102–13
  career selector 185
  opposite number
    14–15

Machiavelli, Niccolò
  119
Mao Zedong 149
Mars 9, 12
mental health day
count
  Aquarius 160
  Aries 22
  Cancer 64
  Capricorn 148
  Gemini 46
  Leo 76
  Libra 106
  Pisces 172
  Sagittarius 130
  Scorpio 118
  Taurus 34
  Virgo 88
Mercury 9, 13
middle management
  96–101
  Aquarius 101
  Leo 99
  Scorpio 100
  Taurus 98
money

Aquarius 158
Aries 20
Cancer 62
Capricorn 146
Gemini 44
Leo 74
Libra 104
Pisces 170
Sagittarius 128
Scorpio 116
Taurus 32
Virgo 86
mutable quality 6, 14,
  138–43

Napoleon Bonaparte
  77

office politics
  Aquarius 162–3
  Aries 24–5
  Cancer 66–7
  Capricorn 150–1
  Gemini 48–9
  Leo 78–9
  Libra 108–9
  Pisces 174–5
  Sagittarius 132–3
  Scorpio 120–1
  Taurus 36–7
  Virgo 90–1
opposite signs 6,
  14–15

parties
  Aquarius 165
  Aries 27
  Cancer 69
  Capricorn 153

Gemini 51
Leo 81
Libra 111
Pisces 177
Sagittarius 135
Scorpio 123
Taurus 39
Virgo 93
passengers
  Aquarius 166
  Aries 28
  Cancer 70
  Capricorn 154
  Gemini 52
  Leo 82
  Libra 112
  Pisces 178
  Sagittarius 136
  Scorpio 124
  Taurus 40
  Virgo 94
Pisces 143, 168–79
  career selector 187
  opposite number
    14–15
Pluto 12

Richard III 107
role models
  Aquarius 161
  Aries 23
  Cancer 65
  Capricorn 149
  Gemini 47
  Leo 77
  Libra 107
  Pisces 173
  Sagittarius 131
  Scorpio 119

Taurus 35
Virgo 89
romance
  Aquarius 164
  Aries 26
  Cancer 68
  Capricorn 152
  Gemini 50
  Leo 80
  Libra 110
  Pisces 176
  Sagittarius 134
  Scorpio 122
  Taurus 38
  Virgo 92

Sagittarius 126–37,
  142
  career selector 186
  opposite number
    14–15
Saturn 9, 10–11
Scorpio 100, 114–25
  career selector 185
  Mars 12
  opposite number
    14–15
sick leave
  Aquarius 158
  Aries 20
  Cancer 62
  Capricorn 146
  Gemini 44
  Leo 74
  Libra 104
  Pisces 170
  Sagittarius 128
  Scorpio 116
  Taurus 32

Virgo 86
slackers 138–43
  Gemini 140
  Pisces 143
  Sagittarius 142
  Virgo 141
Superman 47

Taurus 30–41, 98
  career selector 182
  opposite number
    14–15
teamwork
  Aquarius 166–7
  Aries 28–9
  Cancer 70–1
  Capricorn 154–5
  Gemini 52–3
  Leo 82–3
  Libra 112–13
  Pisces 178–9

Sagittarius 136–7
Scorpio 124–5
Taurus 40–1
Virgo 94–5
timing
  Aquarius 160
  Aries 22
  Cancer 64
  Capricorn 148
  Gemini 46
  Leo 76
  Libra 106
  Pisces 172
  Sagittarius 130
  Scorpio 118
  Taurus 34
  Virgo 88
tricks
  Aquarius 165
  Aries 26, 27
  Cancer 69

Capricorn 152, 153
Gemini 51
Leo 81
Libra 110, 111
Pisces 177
Sagittarius 134,
  135
Scorpio 123
Taurus 39
Virgo 92, 93

Virgo 84–95, 141
  career selector 184
  Mercury 13
  opposite number
    14–15
  Saturn 10

Water 6
  Cancer 57
  Pisces 143

Scorpio 100
watercooler moment
  Aquarius 163
  Aries 25
  Cancer 67
  Capricorn 151
  Gemini 49
  Leo 79
  Libra 109
  Pisces 175
  Sagittarius 133
  Scorpio 121
  Taurus 37
  Virgo 91
workaholics
  Aquarius 158
  Aries 20
  Cancer 62
  Capricorn 146
  Gemini 44
  Leo 74

Libra 104
Pisces 170
Sagittarius 128
Scorpio 116
Taurus 32
Virgo 86
workstations
  Aquarius 159
  Aries 21
  Cancer 63
  Capricorn 147
  Gemini 45
  Leo 75
  Libra 105
  Pisces 171
  Sagittarius 129
  Scorpio 117
  Taurus 33
  Virgo 87

Acknowledgments

The author and publishers would like to thank the following for permission to reproduce photographs:

Bridgeman: Society of Antiquaries, London, UK/The Bridgeman Art Library: page 107.

Corbis: © The Art Archive/Corbis page 77; © Bettmann/CORBIS pages 35, 131, 149, 161, 173; © Stefano Bianchetti/Corbis page 23; © B. Bird/zefa/Corbis page 170; © Fine Art Photographic Library/Corbis page 89; © Jean Michel Foujols/zefa/Corbis page 104; © Hulton-Deutsch Collection/Corbis page 119; © Royalty-Free/Corbis page 44; © Tim Tadder/Corbis page 128; © Bill Varie/Corbis page 158; © Larry Williams/zefa/Corbis page 74.

Getty: The Image Bank/Getty Images pages 20, 32, 146; Photonica/Getty Images pages 62, 86; Stone/Getty Images page 116.